Voices from the Heart

of

God's Inspired Word

To Sylvia and Both
Let this book become for
you a new way of
singing an old, old song,
   Grace and Peace
      Allan

Voices from the Heart

of

God's Inspired Word

Allan Martling

RESOURCE *Publications* · Eugene, Oregon

VOICES FROM THE HEART OF GOD'S INSPIRED WORD

Resource Publications
An Imprint of Wipf and Stock Publishers
199 W. 8th Ave., Suite 3
Eugene, OR 97401

www.wipfandstock.com

ISBN 13: 978-1-61097-027-3

Manufactured in the U.S.A.

Fair Use of *Today's English Version*
American Bible Society, 1976
New York

To my wife, Nancy

Our daughters, Christy and Rebecca

*Our Pastors, Rev. Karen Gale and
Rev. Kari Nicewander*

*And other women and men who have helped me
hear the feminine voice of God*

In Memory of my mother, Margaret

1. Mediator: Happy are they who do not take the arrogant for their guide, nor walk the road the greedy tread, nor take a seat among the scornful; the law of God is their delight, the law their meditation night and day. They prosper in all they do. They are like a tree planted beside a river, which yields its fruit in season and whose leaves never wither. The bigoted are not like this; they are like chaff driven by the wind. When judgment comes, the self-centered shall not stand firm, nor shall the violent stand in the assembly of the good. God watches over the way of the good, but the way of the liar is doomed.

2. Mortal: Why are the nations in turmoil? Why do the people hatch their futile plots? The rulers of the earth stand ready, and they conspire together against God. And God, who sits high and holy, finds them humorous. Then God rebukes them in anger and warns them with holy rage, threatening them with a power that can destroy. But God has lifted me. I remember God calling me, saying, "I am your loving parent and you are my secure child."

Mother: Ask of me what you will. I will give you all the richness of this world as your inheritance, the ends of the earth as your possession. You shall break the unjust powers of others, like shattering a clay pot.

Mediator: Be aware then, you rulers of people; learn your lesson. Worship God with reverence; be in awe and love the Mighty One, lest God become angry and you are struck down at a young age; for God's anger can flare up in a moment. Happy are all who find refuge in God.

3. Mortal: El Shaddai, those who wish to harm me have multiplied! Many rise up against me. Many say of me, "God will not prevail." But You are like a shield to cover me. I cry aloud to You, El Shaddai, and You answer me from on high. I lie down to sleep, and I wake again, for You uphold me. I will not fear all the many who seem to surround me with worry and fear. Rise up, El Shaddai, and save me, O my God. You can strike all my foes and break their hold over me. Yours is the victory, O God, and Your blessings rest upon Your people.

4. Mortal: Answer me when I pray, O God, maintainer of my soul. When I was in trouble, You helped me. Be kind to me now and hear my prayer.

Mother: How long will you people insult Me? How long will you love what is worthless and go after what is false?

Mortal: I remember that You, El Shaddai, have chosen the good for Your own and You hear me when I call to You.

Mediator: Tremble with fear and stop sinning; think deeply about this, when you lie in silence on your beds. Offer faithful sacrifices to El Shaddai and put your trust in Her.

Mortal: There are many who pray, "Give us more blessings, O God. Look on us with kindness!" But the joy that You have given me is more than they will ever have with all their possessions. When I lie down, I go to sleep in peace. You alone, O God, keep me perfectly safe.

5. Mortal: Listen to my words, O God, and hear my sighs. Listen to my cry for help, O my God! I pray to You, O God. You hear my voice in the morning. At sunrise, I offer my prayer and wait for Your answer. You are not a God who is pleased with wrongdoing. You allow no evil in Your presence. You cannot stand the sight of arrogant folk. You hate all wicked people. You destroy all liars and despise the violent and deceitful. But because of Your great love, I can enter Your holy space; I can worship in Your presence and bow down to You in reverence. Sovereign God, I have so many who wish to harm me! Lead me to do Your will. Make Your way plain for me to follow. What violent people say can never be trusted. They only want to destroy. Their words are flattering and smooth, but full of deadly deceit. Condemn and punish them, O God. May their own plots cause their ruin. Drive them out of Your presence because of their many crimes, and their rebellion against You. But all who find safety in You will rejoice. They can always sing for joy. Protect those who love You. Because of You they are truly happy. You bless those who obey You, O God. Your love protects them like safe home.

6. Mortal: Have mercy on me, O God, and do not punish me in Your anger. I am worn out, El Shaddai, have pity on me. Give me strength, for I am completely exhausted, and my whole being is filled with trouble. How long before You help me? Come and save me, O God. In Your mercy rescue me from death. In the world of the dead, I wonder if You are remembered or that anyone would dare praise You. I am worn out with sadness and loss. Every night my bed is damp from my weeping, and my pillow is soaked with tears. I can hardly see, for my eyes are so swollen from the weeping caused by those I feel are attacking me. So I pray for all that I fear to be kept far from me. And I find comfort that You have heard my weeping and have listened to my cries for help. Peace descends upon me when I remember that You, El Shaddai, can hear even my pitiful prayers. So also is that sense that my fears are thrown into confusion and defeat in Your comforting presence!

—

7. Mortal: In You, El Shaddai, I seek refuge. Save me from all who pursue me, the ones who seem like predators, who will carry me away and hurt me. O God, here and now, I confess any wrong that I have done, any way I have betrayed a friend, any time I have failed to show mercy. For I am afraid that if I do not, those whom I fear, may be justified in their chasing me down to revenge the harm I have caused. Stir up Your powerful anger, El Shaddai. Stand against those who want to hurt me for no reason. Let Your justice prevail so that I may once more dwell in the beauty of Your community. For You are the arbiter of all mortals and Your justice defends the innocent. Because You are God, you know our thoughts and desires. You can cease violence and greed in Your time and Your way.

Mediator: El Shaddai is the Protector. She saves those who obey Her. She is fair in Her judgments and does not tolerate wickedness. The corrupt, who do not change their ways, will know the brunt of Her holy fury and will feel the pain of Her discipline. The arrogant do not know this about Her. They think up and plan evil, trouble and deception. They set traps. And in Her wisdom, they are caught in their own cunning. They are punished by their own evil. They are wounded by their own violence. Sing praises for El Shaddai's justice that resolves the brokenness of our lives and shows Her glory.

8. Mortal: Sovereign God, Your greatness is seen in all the world. Your praise reaches up to the heavens and is sung by children and babies. You are safe and secure in the presence of those who despise You. When I look at the sky, which You have made; at the moon and the stars, which You set in their places; what are we, that You think of us? Who are mere mortals, that You care for us? Yet we believe that You have made us inferior only to Yourself and You have crowned us with glory and honor. You appointed us over everything You made. You placed us as stewards of all Creation: sheep, cattle, animals that roam in the wild, and all creatures of the sea. O Sovereign God, Your greatness is evident wherever we are in all the world.

9. Mortal: I will praise You, Sovereign God, with all my heart. I will tell of all the wonderful deeds You have accomplished. I will sing with joy because of You. I will sing praise to You, gentle and wonderful Creator. My enemies sense Your presence and stay away, for they know of Your fair and honest judgments. You treat harshly those who reject You and those who know better, but do wrong anyway. Even their homes are not safe from Your fury. You, O God, are Sovereign for all times. It is Your justice that prevails, and Your commandments that ultimately are followed. You are a refuge for the oppressed and a place of safety in times of trouble. Those who know You, trust You, for You do not abandon anyone who seeks You.

Mediator: Sing praises to El Shaddai, who rules over all people. Tell every nation what She has accomplished. She remembers those who suffer and does not forget their cry. She punishes those who are cruel to the downtrodden.

Mortal: Be merciful to me, El Shaddai. See how I am suffering. Rescue me from death that I may stand before the powerful and speak of all that causes me to praise You. I rejoice because You save me from myself and others.

Mediator: The violent have fallen into the pits they have dug for others. El Shaddai has been revealed by Her fair and faithful judgments, and those who are corrupt are imprisoned in their own scheming. Death is the destiny of all who reject God. And the needy will not always be neglected. The hope of the poor will not be crushed forever.

Mortal: El Shaddai, do not let others defy You! Make them afraid. Make them know that they are only mortal beings.

10. Mortal: O God, hear my prayer and listen to my pleading. Answer me in Your faithfulness. Be generous to me and do not condemn me, remembering that before You, no one is sinless.

Mediator: The wicked are proud of their selfish desires. The greedy curse and reject and do not care about God. In their arrogance, they think God does not matter. Strangely, the violent are often successful in this world, and they cannot understand God's judgments. So they sneer and think they will never fail nor ever be in trouble. Their speech is filled with curses, lies, and threats. They are quick to speak hateful, evil words. These folk hide in their communities waiting to do great harm to innocent people like the predators that they are. They lie in wait for the poor, to catch and oppress them. The helpless victims lie crushed by the brute strength of those who think that God doesn't care; that God's eyes are closed and will never see this oppression.

Mortal: Sovereign God, punish those hurtful people. Remember the ones who suffer. How can the violent go on thinking You will not punish them? But You do see. You take notice of the trouble and suffering, the heartache and degradation. You are ready to help those who are faithful to You. You have always helped the needy in Your time and Your way. I pray that You will break the power of the oppressors. Punish them for the wrong they do until they cease.

Mediator: God is Sovereign over all principalities and powers, even death itself. Those who worship other gods will vanish from the earth. God will listen to the prayers of the lowly and will give them courage. God will hear the cries of the oppressed and the orphans and will judge in their favor. God will bring peace!

11. Mortal: I trust in the Sovereign God for my safety. How foolish for you to say, "Fly away, like a bird, to the mountains." The predators are out to get me as I walk in fear. There is nothing I can do when everything falls apart.

Mediator: El Shaddai is all powerful on high. She watches people everywhere and knows what they are doing. She examines the good and the bigoted alike. She rages over those who love violence. She can send fire and hot coals and a scorching dry wind to destroy the greedy thoughts of people. El Shaddai is merciful and just. She loves good deeds, and those who act faithfully will live in Her presence.

12. Mortal: Help us, O God! There don't seem to be any good folk remaining, nor can one who is honest be found. All of us lie to one another. We deceive each other with flattery. Silence these arrogant tongues, O God. Close our boastful mouths that say, "With our words we get what we want. We will say what we wish, and no one can stop us."

Mother: I will intervene, because the needy are oppressed and the persecuted groan in pain. I will give them the well-being for which they pray.

Mediator: The promises of El Shaddai can be trusted. They are as genuine as silver that is refined to its highest purity. She shall lift up the poor and guard them forever from this perverse and hard-hearted generation.

13. Mortal: O my God, will you forget me forever? How much longer will you hide Yourself from me? How must I endure trouble? How long will sorrow fill my heart day and night? How long will my enemies triumph over me? Answer me, El Shaddai, for You are my only hope. Bring me into the light, lest I sleep in death. Do not let the ones, who wish to harm me, overcome my resistance or take more advantage of my weakness. I rely on Your constant love. I will sing for joy when You draw me into Your safe embrace, as You have before.

14. Mediator: Only fools think that there is no God. They are corrupt and act in awful ways. None of them does anything good. El Shaddai considers them from on high, searching for any mortal who bows down to worship Her. But the foolish have all gone astray; every one of them is empty and broken.

Mother: Don't these foolish souls know? How can all these arrogant folk be so ignorant? They live by cunning and dishonesty, taking from others what does not belong to them, and they never truly pray to Me.

Mediator: But the time will come when they will see that El Shaddai sides with the faithful and the humble. The efforts to destroy the poor will be frustrated. She protects her own. It is El Shaddai's people who will be lead to salvation. The blessed and precious people will rejoice when She lifts them and restores them.

Honor Her, you descendants of Jacob and Rachael. Worship Her, you blessed people. She does not neglect the poor or ignore their suffering. She does not turn away from them. El Shaddai answers their prayers in Her time and Her way." In the full assembly, I will praise You, El Shaddai, for what You have done. In the presence of those who worship You, I will offer the sacrifices I promised.

Mediator: The poor will eat as much as they want. Those who come to El Shaddai will praise Her. May they prosper forever; all nations will remember Her. From all directions they will turn to Her, and all races will worship Her. She is Sovereign over all people. The proud will bow down before Her. Future generations will serve Her. Mortals will speak of Her to coming generations. People not yet born will be told, "El Shaddai saves the people!"

---

23. Mortal: Because You, El Shaddai, are more than a healthy and loving parent to me, I have everything I need. You embrace me in Your safe home. You provide me with good water to drink. You nurture and strengthen me. You guide me in the way I should live, as You promised You would. Even if I face death itself, I will not be afraid, El Shaddai, for You are with me. Your power and protection surround me. You prepare abundant and nutritious meals for me, even when I am troubled and in danger. You always welcome me into Your graceful presence, and my cup of joy overflows. I know that Your goodness and mercy will follow me as long as I live. I will live forever in the comfort of Your loving presence!

24. Mediator: The universe and all that is in it belong to El Shaddai, as do the earth, and all who live on it. She built it on the deep waters, beneath the earth, and laid its foundations in the ocean depths. Who has the right to go up Her holy hill? Who may enter into Her presence? Those who seek to be pure in act and in thought, who do not worship gods of their own making, or make false promises. El Shaddai will bless the faithful and save them. She will declare them innocent. Such are the people who come to God, who come into the presence of the God of our ancestors. Swing wide the mighty gate, open the ancient door of your soul, and the Sovereign One will enter. Who is She? She is mighty in her caring and humble in Her power. Open the tightly closed door of Your soul, mind, and strength. Who is El Shaddai? The One who is triumphant in Her gentleness!

25. Mortal: O God, I open my heart to You. In Your love, I put all my trust. Do not let me be mocked. Do not let my adversaries triumph over me. Vindicate the confidence of all those who wait for You, but shame those who deceive others without reason. Teach me Your ways, O God, so I can live according to Your truth, for You are my God, who saves me. I will always trust You. I remember Your kindness and constant love, which You have shown from long ago. I confess the sins of my younger years, and in Your constant love and goodness, ask for Your mercy.

Mediator: Because El Shaddai is righteous and good, She teaches sinners the path they should follow. She leads the humble in the faithful ways and teaches them Her will. With faithfulness and love, She leads all who keep Her Covenant and obey Her commands.

Mortal: Forgive my sins, in your love for me. My sins are many. They are . . .

Mediator: Those who obey El Shaddai will learn from Her the path they should follow. They will always have enough, and their children will inherit the blessing. She is the friend of those who obey Her, and She affirms Her Covenant with them.

Mortal: I look to El Shaddai for help at all times, and She rescues me from danger. Turn to me, O God, and be merciful to me, because I am lonely and weak. Relieve me of my worries, and save me from all my troubles. Consider my distress and suffering, and forgive all my sins. See all my troubles and how much they bear down on me. Protect me and save me. Keep me from disaster. I seek You for safety. May what I have done in goodness and honesty preserve me, because I trust in You, O God. And from all their troubles, O God, save all Your precious people.

---

26. Mortal: Dear God, judge me innocent because I do what is good and trust You completely. Examine me and test me, Divine Lover. Judge my desires and thoughts. Your constant love is my guide. Your faithfulness always leads me. I do not keep company with worthless people. I have nothing to do with those who say one thing and do another. I hate the company of those who are schemers, abusers, and the corrupt. O God, look upon my clean hands as a sign of my innocence, as I approach Your altar in worship, singing a hymn of thanksgiving and telling others of all Your wonderful deeds. I love being present in Your Holy Place, where I sense Your glory. Do not destroy me with those who betray Your love. Spare me from those who harass the lives of others, those who oppress the poor and are always ready to take bribes. I maintain that I do what is good. Be merciful to me and save me! Then I can be safe from all dangers. Then in the assembly of Your people I will praise You, merciful God.

---

27. **Mortal:** The Sovereign God is my light and my salvation. I will fear no one. El Shaddai protects me from all danger. I will never be afraid. When unjust people attack me, and others devour me with slander, they will stumble and fall. Though they surround me I will not be afraid. I will always trust God. In my prayers, I pray that I may live close to El Shaddai's presence all of my life, and to ask for Her guidance. In times of trouble, She will shelter me, keeping me safe in Her home. She will set me firmly upon the rock of Her purposes, so that I cannot be shaken. I will always be filled with the joy of Her presence and sing praises to El Shaddai! I am grateful that She answers me in prayer. When She calls me to worship, I enter into worship, joyfully knowing that my Savior does not abandon me. She has heard my prayers, "Don't be angry with me! Don't turn Your servant away! Don't leave or abandon me, my Helper. My mother and father abandoned me, but You will take care of me. Teach me, El Shaddai, what You want me to do, and lead me along a safe pathway. Don't abandon me to my enemies,

within and around me. I know that I will live to see Your goodness in my lifetime."

Mediator: Trust in God. Have faith; do not despair. Trust in El Shaddai.

---

28. Mortal: When I call to You, O God my Strength, do not turn away from my plea! If Your response is only silence, I will be completely devastated. Hear me when I cry to You for help, when I raise my hands to You on high. Do not condemn me with the wicked; with those who look out only for themselves and trample on the unfortunate; who are hardhearted toward the lowly and outcast. Punish them for what they do; for their arrogant ways. Give them the punishment they deserve. They completely disregard what You are doing in life. So I am praising You, for You have heard my cry for help. You, O God, protect and defend me. I trust in You. You give me help and make me glad. I praise You with joyful songs.

Mediator: El Shaddai protects Her people. She defends those who are called to lead others. She saves and blesses those who are precious and valuable, taking care of them forever!

---

29. Mediator: The heavenly beings and all angels praise God's glory and power, bowing down before the Holy One's presence. The Word of El Shaddai is heard on the waters, like thunder; Her Word reverberates in might and majesty. Her power can break mighty trees and make mountains jump like calves or leap like a young bull. The Word of God flashes like lightning, illuminating even the wilderness. The power of God can bend mighty oaks and strip the leaves from their branches. Glory to God, all people! El Shaddai rules over the deep waters. She is Sovereign forever. She gives strength to the people and blesses them with peace.

30. Mortal: I praise You, El Shaddai, for rescuing, and lifting me up. You healed me when I cried to You for help. You kept me from dying. My life was slipping away, but You brought me back from the edge.

Mediator: Sing praise to El Shaddai, all faithful people. Remember what the Holy One has done and give Her thanks. Her anger lasts only a moment. But Her goodness lasts for a lifetime. Tears may flow in the night, but joy comes in the morning.

Mortal: In my security, I feel safe because of El Shaddai's gentle strength and protection. But when She seems far away, I feel vulnerable and afraid. Then I call out in prayer, "Help me, O God. What will You accomplish by letting me die? If I die, can I praise You? Can I proclaim Your goodness in the grave? Hear me, O God, and be merciful!" And in great mercy I can rejoice that She changed my sadness and fright into a joyful dance. I pray, "You, El Shaddai, have taken away my sorrow and surrounded me with joy. I will sing Praise to You. You have shown me Your mercy. I will give thanks to You, O God!"

31. Mortal: Sovereign God, when I feel close to disaster, I pray to You for protection. You are a righteous God. Save me, I pray! Hear me! Be my refuge to protect me, my defense to save me. Guide me and lead me as You have promised. Keep me safe from the dangers that await me. I place myself in Your care, trusting in Your saving and faithful power. I will separate myself from those who follow false values. I will reject all the ways society worships the things and values they have created. I will trust only You and rejoice in Your constant love. You know of my suffering and my troubles. You know when I am surrounded. Save me to live free from fear. When I am troubled, O God, my eyes tire from so much crying and I get completely worn out. It is as though my life is shorter because of all my weeping and sorrow. At times, it is like my very bones are wasting away. And around me, it seems as though even my neighbors treat me with contempt. When I am troubled, it is as though my friends are afraid of me. When they see me in the street, it seems like they turn away and run from me. In my deepest troubles, I wonder if I am dead, for people act like they have forgotten me. I feel discarded, with people whispering about me, and everywhere I go, I am afraid. But my trust is in You, Sovereign God. I find comfort knowing that I am always in Your care, saving me from my enemies within and around me. My prayers are that You look upon Your servant with kindness, saving me in Your abundant love and mercy. I pray that I may not be disgraced. I have even been known to pray that others who dishonor me be punished as I would have them suffer. At all times I give You thanks, Sovereign God, for the wonder and goodness that You show to the faithful. I rejoice in how securely You protect those who trust You. You hide them in the safety of Your presence, safe from plots, rumors, insults, and violence. I praise You, O God, for Your abundant love. I give thanks that even when I almost give up hope, You hear my cries and surround me with Your strength.

Mediator: Love God, you faithful people. The Sovereign God protects the faithful but punishes the arrogant as they deserve. Be strong, be courageous, all you who hope in God.

﹏

32. **Mediator:** Happy are those whose sins are forgiven, whose wrongs are pardoned. Happy are they whom God does not accuse of doing wrong and who are free from all deceit.

Mortal: When I did not confess my sins, O God, I was worn out from crying all day long. Day and night, You punished me. My strength was completely drained, as moisture is dried up by the summer heat. Then I confessed my sins to You, O God. I did not conceal my wrongdoings. I decided to confess them to You, and You forgave all my sins. So all Your loyal people should pray to You in times of need. When a great flood of trouble comes rushing in, it will not reach them. You are my hiding place. You will save me from trouble. I sing aloud of Your salvation, because You protect me.

Mother: I will teach you the way you should go. I will instruct you and advise you. Don't be stupid like a horse or a mule, which must be controlled with a bit and bridle to make it submit.

Mediator: The wicked will have to suffer, but those who trust in God are protected with constant love. You who are good and faithful, be glad and rejoice because of what God is doing. You who live in obedience to God, shout for joy.

﹏

33. **Mediator:** Good and faithful folk, shout for joy for what El Shaddai has accomplished. Praise Her, all you that obey Her. Give thanks to Her with harps and stringed instru-

ments. Sing a new song to Her. Play the harp with skill and shout for joy. The words of El Shaddai are true and can be trusted. She loves what is good and just. Her constant love fills the earth. By God's command, the heavens were created as were the sun, moon, and stars. And all the seas were gathered into one place. Have reverence for El Shaddai, all the earth. Honor Her, all people of the world. When She speaks, Creation happens and newness appears. She frustrates the schemes of nations and keeps them from carrying out their plans. But Her will and way shall endure forever. Happy is the nation who follows God. Happy are God's own people. She considers it all from on high and sees mere mortals. She knows their thoughts and all that they do. Leaders do not win because of powerful armies, nor do soldiers prevail because of their strength. War machines are useless for true victory; their great strength cannot save. El Shaddai watches over those who have reverence for Her, those who trust in Her constant love. She saves them from death. She keeps them alive in times of famine.

Mortal: We put our hope in El Shaddai. She is our protector and our help. We are glad because of Her. We trust in Her holy name. May Your constant love be with us, El Shaddai, as we put our hope in You.

---

34. Mortal: I will always thank El Shaddai. I will never stop praising Her. I will praise Her for all that She has done. May all who are oppressed listen and be glad! Proclaim, with me, Her greatness. Let us praise Her name together! I prayed to El Shaddai, and She answered me. She freed me from all my fears.

Mediator: The oppressed look to El Shaddai and are glad. They will never be disappointed. The helpless call to Her, and She answers. She saves them from all their troubles. Her angel guards those who have reverence for Her, and She rescues them from danger. Find out for yourself how good El Shaddai is. Happy are those who find safety with Her. Have reverence for El Shaddai, all people. Those who obey Her have all they need. Everyone goes hungry for lack of food, but those who obey Her lack nothing good. Come, my young friends, and listen to me. I will teach you to have reverence for God. Would you like to enjoy life? Do you want long life and happiness? Then keep from speaking in an evil way and from telling lies. Turn away from dishonesty and do good. Strive for peace with all your heart. El Shaddai watches over the faithful and good and listens to their cries. She opposes those who are wicked and disgusting; so when they die, they are soon forgotten. The faithful and good call to Her, and She listens. She rescues them from all their troubles. She is near to those who are discouraged. She saves those who have lost all hope. Good people suffer many troubles, but El Shaddai saves them from disaster. She preserves them completely. Evil ways will ultimately destroy those who hate what is faithful and good. El Shaddai will save Her people. Those who go to Her for protection will be spared.

---

35. Mortal: At a time when I am surrounded by many troubles, I pray that God may come to my rescue with all power, glory, and majesty. I pray that God may save me from defeat and disgrace. May God's presence make my troubles like straw blown in the wind. May God's angels make those who pursue me slip and fall. Without any reason, I have been placed in great danger. I pray for God's justice to roll, bringing peace and hope. Then I will be glad because God has saved me. With all my heart, I will pray, "O God, there is no one like You. You protected my weakness in the presence of overwhelming odds as you protect the poor from the oppressor." Evil folk testified against me and accused me of crimes I know nothing about. They paid me back evil for good, and I sank in despair. But when they were sick, I dressed in mourning. I deprived myself of food. I prayed with my head bowed low, as I would pray for a friend. I went around bent over in mourning as one who mourns for a mother. But when I was in trouble, they were all glad, and gathered around to make fun of me. Strangers would strike me. Like those who would mock a crippled soul, they would glare at me with hate. I pray, "How much longer, O God, will You just look on? Rescue me from these attacks. Save my life from these predators. Then I will thank You in the assembly of Your people. I will praise You before them all. Don't let these liars gloat over my defeat. Don't let those who hate me for no reason smirk with delight over my sorrow. They do not speak in a friendly way. Instead they invent all kinds of lies about peace-loving people. They shout accusations at me. But You, O God, have seen this. So don't be silent, O God. Don't keep Yourself far away. Rouse Yourself and defend me. Rise up and plead my cause. You are righteous, O God. Declare me innocent. Don't let my enemies gloat over me. Don't let them think they have prevailed as they wanted. May those who gloat over my suffering be completely confused and defeated; may those who claim to be better than I am be covered with shame and disgrace." I pray, "May those who come to my assistance, shout for joy and say over and

at and good. May they shout
on. Then I will proclaim Your
You all day long! Amen."

e hearts of the wicked, sinful-
th no fear of God. The uncar-
tter themselves with their own
are held accountable, they do
er lie and testify falsely against
der the strength of wisdom. In
est to continue their corruption
hey welcome all that is harmful;
. But El Shaddai's unfailing love
r righteousness is high like lofty
s are deep like the great canyons.
El Shadda... on with unfailing love. Wise mortals seek refuge in the shadow of Her wings. How precious
is Her generous affection. The faithful are filled with the
rich and plenty of Her abundance. To quench their thirst,
She grants them water as from a flowing stream, for She is
the fountain of life. All their days are filled with Her radiant
light. El Shaddai's love will never fail, and Her justice will
continue toward all who honestly follow Her. No treachery
will come near them, nor shall they know wickedness. But
the arrogant will be defeated, never to rise.

37. Mediator: Do not strive to outdo the self-centered or
emulate those who only do harm to themselves and others. Like grass, they will soon wither and fade in the heat
of summer. Trust in God and do good. Find a place to call

home and have peace. Depend on El Shaddai, and She will grant you your heart's desire. Commit your life to Her and trust in Her, and She will respond. She will make your goodness shine clear as the day. The justice of your cause will radiate like the sun at noon. Wait quietly for Her; be patient when you cannot find Her. Do not try to outdo the successful nor envy those who seem to prosper. Give up any thoughts of being angry. Do not compete in evil-doing. For God's ways will attend to those who visit the lowly with fear. God will give them their punishment. All those who hope in El Shaddai shall find a safe and abundant home. As for the gossipers, their time is limited. Their place will be empty. But the humble will enjoy prosperity. The gossipers will mutter against all who are good and grind their teeth when they think of goodness. But El Shaddai will laugh at them, knowing their time is short. The violent rage against the poor and needy, the honest folk; they shall die by their own violence. Better is a little of the good than the great wealth of the greedy. El Shaddai upholds the good but will break the strength of the corrupt. She knows each day of the life of good folk, and Her inheritance shall last forever. When times are bad, the good will not be distressed. There shall be enough in times of famine. But for the selfish, their family will have to beg for bread. Those who reject the ways of God shall disappear like smoke. Those who borrow and never pay back are unlike those who are generous givers. All whom El Shaddai has blessed will find a safe home, but those who curse Her shall be destroyed. It is El Shaddai who directs the steps of mortals. She holds them firm and watches over their pathways. Though they may fall, She will not let them be embarrassed. She will lift them up. All ages of faithful have been cared for like this. Every day they are being led in such a gentle way that their lives become a blessing. Turn from evil and do good; live at peace forever. El Shaddai is a lover of justice and will not turn away loyal servants. But the lawless and those who refuse to follow the commandments will be destroyed. El Shaddai's faithful and humble servants shall live in peace forever.

38. Mortal: Why do you punish me in anger, O God? Why do You chasten me in Your fury? I am wounded, and I feel the weight of Your presence upon me. There is no integrity in me, because of Your wrath. There is no health in my body, because of my sins. I am over my head in guilt. My faults are a burden too heavy for me. I am wounded by my own foolishness. I am utterly bowed down with grief, bent over and stricken with sorrow. My soul is sick, and I am completely crushed. I moan in pain because my heart is full of turmoil. My God, You know my longings. My sighs are no secret to You. My heart is weak, and my strength deserts me. The light in my eyes is snuffed out. The sickness of my soul drives my friends away. My neighbors and family keep their distance. Too many don't seem to care about me at all. Others seek to hurt me, to trap me in their deceit. But I turn a deaf ear and keep my mouth shut. I act like someone who can't hear. Meanwhile, I wait for You, O God. How I hope You will help me. Do not let my troubles destroy me. I am in constant pain, ready to sink into the depths. I confess my foolishness and am truly sorry for my sins. Still, my demons are strong and lively, while I feel week and anxious. I am hurt by those who treat me with dishonesty, even when they think they are helping me. Though I am good to them, their words and deeds beat me down. My efforts to do what

seems good, appear to be useless. Do not rebuke me, O
God. Be always close to me and assist me! You are my only
hope for healing and safety.

---

39. Mortal: I resolved to be careful about what I do and
not let my tongue make me sin. When those who twist my
words were near, I would not even say anything good. Even
so, my suffering only grew worse, and I was overcome with
anxiety. The more I thought, the more troubled I became.
I could not keep from wondering if I were going to die. I
prayed to God about my life, "Sovereign God, I am still very
young. Does my life seem worthless to You? I know that I
am no more than a puff of wind, no more than a shadow.
I seem to work hard for nothing, gathering wealth for un-
known reasons. What then can I hope for, O God? I put my
hope in You. Save me from all my sins, and don't let fools
make fun of me. I will keep quiet. I will not say a word. Are
You the One who is making me suffer like this? If so, I pray
that my suffering may end. I have been brought low by this
punishment. I know that You can punish me for my sins
and You can destroy the things that I love. I know that to
You, I am no more than a bubble in a huge fountain. Hear
my prayer, Sovereign God, and listen to my cry. Come to
my aid when I weep. Like all those who have gone before
me, I am only in this mortal life for a short time. Would it
be better if You left me alone? Would I be happier, if only for
a short time? Amen."

---

40. Mortal: I waited patiently for El Shaddai, and She listened and answered me. She drew me up from my desola-

tion. I was freed from the muck in which I was trapped. She set my feet on firm ground and made my way secure. She gave me a new and joyful song to sing. As a result, many have seen this and turned in trust to Her. Blessed are all those who trust in Her, who do not trust the arrogant or follow corrupt leaders. El Shaddai has done great acts for us all. Her works and designs are marvelous. None can compare with El Shaddai. To tell all Her goodness would be utterly beyond me. She does not demand sacrifices and offerings to buy Her favor. She opens our ears and our hearts and longs to hear us say, "Here am I as a sacrifice to You, O God! I delight in doing Your will. Your commandments are written on my heart." I have proclaimed Your justice and goodness, El Shaddai, to great assemblies. I cannot restrain my lips. I have never made a secret of Your saving help. I speak out and proclaim Your saving faithfulness. I do not conceal Your love or truth from any congregation. Do not withhold Your tender mercies from me. In loving kindness and faithfulness, keep constant watch over me. With so much sadness and brokenness around me, I can hardly hold my head up. I am surrounded by evils that are more than the hairs on my head. Look with favor on me, El Shaddai, and hurry to help me. Drive away all my troubles and those who delight in them; may those who taunt me be thoroughly ashamed. But let all who seek You experience Your grace and rejoice in Your saving presence. Let all those who love Your holiness magnify You. In times when I am poor and needy, I know You remember me. You are my helper and deliverer, El Shaddai. I wait patiently for You.

41. Mediator: Happy are those who are concerned for the poor. The Sovereign God will help them when they are in trouble. El Shaddai will protect them and preserve their lives. She will make them happy. She will not abandon them to the power of others. She will help them when they are sick and will restore them to health.

Mortal: I have sinned against You, O God. Be merciful to me and heal me. My enemies say cruel things about me. They want me to die and be forgotten. Those who visit me are not sincere. They gather bad news about me. They say that I am fatally ill and I will never leave my bed again. Even my best friend, the one I trusted most, the one who shared my food, has turned against me. Be merciful to me, El Shaddai, and restore my health. Then I will pay my enemies back. They will no longer prevail over me. I know that You are pleased with me. Help me, for I am Your faithful servant. Keep me in your presence forever. I praise You, El Shaddai. I praise You, now and forever!

<hr/>

42. Mortal: Like a deer thirsting for flowing streams, my soul longs for You, Sovereign God, the true and living God. When will I be able to be in Your presence? My tears flow constantly, while others question why I seek You. My heart breaks when I remember the past. I used to lead people in processions of praise. Together, we sang songs of worship and celebrated the great feasts, shouting songs of praise to You. Why am I so sad now? Why am I so troubled? Once again, I will put my hope in El Shaddai and praise You, my Creator and my Redeemer! In this strange land where I find myself, I feel that my heart is breaking. I turn my thoughts and prayers to You, as waves of sorrow flow over my soul. May El Shaddai's love be constant during the day so that I may have a song at night! I pray, "Why have You forgotten me? Why must I go on suffering from the cruelty of my enemies? I am crushed by their insults as they keep on asking me about Your silence and absence. Why am I so sad? Why am I so troubled? Hear my prayer." I will put my hope in El Shaddai! Once more I will praise Her, my Creator and Redeemer.

43. Mortal: O God, declare me innocent and defend my cause against the hard-hearted. Deliver me from those who are lying and unjust people. O God, in You is my strength. Will You withhold Your power from me? Why must I go on suffering from the cruelty of others? Send Your light and truth to lead me. Bring me back into your gentle presence where You live. Then I will praise and honor You, for You are the source of my joy. I will play instruments of celebration and sing praise to You, O God. So, why am I sad? Why am I troubled? I will put my hope in You, O God. Once again, I will praise You, my Creator and Redeemer.

44. Mortal: With my own ears I have heard it, O God. Our ancestors have told us about the great deeds You have accomplished in their lives. You drove out the natives and established Your people in their land. You punished other nations and caused Your own to prosper. Your people did not conquer the land with their strength. It was Your power and Your presence that showed everyone that You loved us.

You are the Sovereign God over all principalities and powers, even death itself. You have saved us from our enemies and defeated those who were against us. We will always praise You and give thanks to You forever. But now, You have rejected us and let us be defeated. You no longer are present with us in our conflicts with other nations. So now we run from others. And they take what is ours for themselves. You allow us to be destroyed, and You scatter us far from our homes. We find ourselves as slaves, owning little of value. Others observe all this and mock us and laugh at us. We have become a joke among the nations. They shake their heads at us in scorn. I feel this disgrace. I am covered with shame from hearing the sneers and insults of those who hate us. All this has happened to us, even though we continue to worship You. We maintain that we are loyal to You. Yet You have left us in a wilderness, and we stagger in the gloom. If we stopped worshiping You and prayed to a foreign god, You would know it, for you know our secret thoughts and actions. It is for Your sake that we are being killed all the time. It is like we are being treated like sheep to be slaughtered. Wake up, O God! Why does it seem that You are sleeping? Rouse Yourself. Don't reject us forever. Stop hiding from us! Remember our suffering and trouble! We fall crushed to the ground. We lie defeated in the dust. Come to our aid! Because of Your constant love, save us!

45. **Mortal:** Beautiful words fill my mind as I compose this song for a faithful servant leader. Like the pen of a good writer, my tongue is ready with a poem. "You are good-looking and an eloquent speaker. God has richly blessed

you. Use what God has given you in all that you do. Prevail in the defense of truth and justice. Your strength is also a gift from God. Because of your ability, others will have great respect for you. The realm of God will prosper in your time. You lead others with justice. You love what is good and hate what is corrupt. That is why God continues to bless you, pouring out abundant blessings. Your blessings are the adulation of fine musicians, and your family is held high by others. Rich people will bring you gifts and try to win your favor. All who are close to you rejoice with joy and gladness. May your family continue this blessing; may your gifts of leadership pass to them in their generation. May your love of truth and justice spread far and wide; may this song keep your fame alive so many will praise you for a long time."

46. **Mediator:** Our refuge and strength is in God, who is always willing to help in times of trouble. Therefore, we will not be afraid, even when the whole world is turned upside down and nothing seems to have order any more. For the river of God's peace flows through us, a stream of clear water that cleanses our fearful souls. Because God dwells within our hearts, we will not lose our courage. God's love is with us, like the sun, every day. Though there are wars and calamities among the nations, God's word can be heard above the turmoil. The Sovereign God is with us. The God of our ancestors is our safe home. I can show you how wonderful God is. God can bring peace where there is violence. God can turn weapons into machines that till the soil and lift the lives of people.

Mother: End domination over the poor and all violence. Know My Sovereign Power over all people, over all nations, over all the world.

Mediator: This God is among us. This is the God of our ancestors.

---

47. Mediator: With joy, all people; clap your hands. Praise God with loud songs. Hold El Shaddai in awe. She is Sovereign, ruling in all the world. She helps people to prevail in trouble and is the inspiration of nations. She chose for us to live in this place, blessing us out of Her love. All people praise Her on high with shouts of joy and the sound of trumpets. Sing praise to El Shaddai. Sing praise to the One who can be found in all the world. Praise Her with songs. From on high She leads all people. All leaders gather together as did our ancestors. She is stronger than all that mortal groups can muster. She is more powerful than standing armies. She is Sovereign over all principalities and powers, even death itself.

---

48. Mediator: Now hear this! The Sovereign God is great and is to be highly praised. Within the holy cities of the world, God rules, bringing joy to all around. There is safety within the communities of God. Even powerful leaders are in awe of God's mighty strength. It is much more than they are or have. God's reign is feared by many. It brings about pain, like that of childbirth, or fear of ships tossed in a mighty storm at sea. This news gets around. Many have experienced God's power themselves. Communities who live within this power can live in safety. God's presence is constant love. God is praised by people all over the world. God rules with justice, making the peoples joyful in peace. God's judgments bring fairness and freedom from fear. People of these cities, remember how it is with God protecting and directing us. Tell it to those who long to know and to the next generations. God creates this kind of peace and wellbeing. God's reign will be forever.

49. Mediator: Listen to what I have to say, all people everywhere. Hear these words, rich and poor, powerful and powerless, young and old everywhere. What I am about to say is deep, as I speak words of God-given understanding. Do not be afraid in times of danger, when oppression and disaster threaten. What can those who trust in riches, which they have stolen, do, except to boast of their great wealth? By your own efforts, you cannot redeem yourselves. Indeed, no one can escape death; even the lives of the wise end in death. All must leave this earth and their wealth. Their graves become their homes where they will stay, though they once owned lands and more. Even greatness cannot keep mortal souls from death. See what happens to those who trust in themselves and who are satisfied with their own wealth? They too will die. But for the good and faithful people, God will take away the power of death, which hangs over the unfaithful. For those who trust in God, the fear of death will be no more. So don't be envious when others become wealthy. They cannot take it with them beyond the grave. Even if folk are satisfied with life and praised because of their successes, they will join their ancestors in death. Even greatness cannot keep mortals from death.

50. Mediator: The strong and gentle El Shaddai speaks, calling the whole earth from east to west. She shines in faithful communities. Though She can be found in silence, She is present in raging fire and furious storms. Heaven and earth are Her witnesses. She is the judge over all people.

Mother: Gather My faithful people to Me, those who made a Covenant with Me by offering a sacrifice.

Mediator: The heavens proclaim that El Shaddai is a righteous judge.

Mother: Listen, My people, and I will speak. I will testify against you. I am God, your God. I do not reprimand you because of your sacrifices and good service in My name. I do not need the things that you give Me, for all the treasures of the earth are Mine. The world and everything in it belongs to Me! Do you think I need what you offer Me? Do I spend money or live confined in the sanctuaries you build? I prefer that your sacrifice be the gift of gratitude to Me. I rejoice in your solemn promises. Then I will save you in the day of disaster, and you will praise Me. Listen to this, you who ignore Me. Why do you recite My Commandments? Why should you talk about My Covenant? You refuse to let Me lead you. You reject My commands. You become the friend of every thief you see, and you associate yourselves with those who violate others. You are always ready to speak evil and never hesitate to tell lies. You are ready to accuse even members of your own family and find fault with them. You continue to do this, and I have remained silent. You think that I approve. But I will punish you and make My thoughts perfectly clear. Listen to this, you who ignore Me, or I will destroy you. Because I am God, and there is no other, there will be no one to save you. Giving Me thanks is the sacrifice that honors Me. Do this, and I will surely save all those who obey Me.

⸻

51. Mortal: O God, dear merciful God, because of Your constant love, wipe away all my sins! I confess the faults that I know I have committed and the ones I commit in my ignorance. These are all sins against You and You alone. You are justified in condemning me in Your righteous judgment. I have been this way all my life. You, O God, require that I am sincere and truthful. Fill my heart, mind, and soul with Your will and Your way. Remove my sin, and I will be clean. Wash me, and I will be pure. Let me hear the sounds of joy and gladness. Though You crush me and break me, in redeeming me, I will rejoice once again. Create a pure heart in me, O God. Put a new and faithful spirit in me. Do not banish me from Your presence. Do not take Your sustaining Spirit away from me. Give me the joy that comes from Your Salvation. Make me willing to obey You. Then I will be able to teach others about Your mercy, and they will turn back to You. Spare my life, O God, and save me. Then I can gladly proclaim Your righteousness. Help me to speak, O God, and I will praise You. Then I will teach other transgressors Your ways, that they may return, with me, to You. Deliver me from being destructive, O God. You alone can save me from my sinful behavior. O God, open my lips, and I will proclaim Your praise. My tongue shall sing aloud of Your loving generosity. You do not delight in offerings and gifts given to secure Your favor. We honor You through the sacrifice of a humble spirit and a confessing heart.

52. Mediator: Why do you boast, foolish people, of all the wrong that you do? God's love is eternal. You make plans to ruin others. Your tongues speak words that deeply wound others. You are always inventing lies. You love evil more than good and falsehood more than truth. You love to hurt people with your self-serving arrogance. Now hear this: El Shaddai will ruin you forever. She will take hold of you and uproot you from your safe place. She will remove you from the life that you live. Good people will see Her power and be in awe. Then they will laugh at you, seeing ones who did not depend on El Shaddai for safety. You trusted instead in your great wealth and looked for security in being wicked.

Mortal: I am like an ancient tree growing in El Shaddai's presence. I trust in Her constant love forever and ever. I will always thank Her for all She has accomplished. I will proclaim Her righteousness.

53. Mediator: Fools think to themselves that there is no God. They are all corrupt, and act terribly. None of them does anything good. El Shaddai is aware of all mortals. From on high, She sees if there are any who are wise, who bend their knees in holy worship. But the foolish ones have all turned away. They are all equally bad. Not one of them does any good for the poor or outcast children of Hers.

Mother: Don't they know? Are these evil-doers ignorant? They live by robbing My people, and they never pray to Me.

Mediator: The foolish ones will become terrified as they have never been before. El Shaddai will completely remove any evidence of their presence. She has rejected them. Her humble, faithful people will prevail over them.

Mortal: I pray that El Shaddai's precious people will prevail. How happy the poor and the outcasts will be when She will make them prosper once again.

---

54. Mortal: Save me by Your power, O God. Set me free by Your strength. Hear my prayer, O God. Listen to my words! For detractors have risen against me, cruel people who seek to wound me. They don't even care about You, O God! You are my helper and defender, O God. I pray that You may bring all these attackers to ruin and destroy all their malice. Gladly I offer You praise and thanksgiving, O God, for You are merciful and just! You deliver me from heartache and let me find security in times of trouble.

---

55. Mortal: Hear my prayer, O God. Don't turn away from my humble cry. Consider my words and answer them. I am worn out by my worries. I am terrified by the threats of others. I am crushed by the oppression of the wicked; they constantly bring me trouble. They are always angry in their hate of me. I am terrified to the point of fearing for my life. All I feel is terror and trembling. I am completely overcome. I wish I had the wings of a bird, so I could fly away and find rest. I would fly far away and make my home in a silent wilderness. I would find a shelter from these raging storms. I see violence and riots all around. My world is filled with the sounds of crime and trouble, night and day. There is destruction everywhere. The streets are full of oppression and fraud. The trouble comes not from outsiders and strangers. Rather, my acquaintances cause so much trouble. They know who I am. They live close by. They are my colleagues and close friends, the people in my faith community. What is most distressing is the damage being done by people I know very well. I call to You, El Shaddai, for help, knowing that You will save me. Morning, noon, and night, my complaints and groans go to You in prayer. I know that You will hear my cries. In Your own time and way, I will be brought back to safety, free from all these battles. El Shaddai, You are more powerful than all other powers. Even the most difficult hearts can be changed by Your will; as when my former companion attacked his friends and broke his promises, when his words dripped with the hatred in his heart. Even in these times, Your redeeming strength prevails. So I leave my troubles with You, El Shaddai, and You will be my strength and courage. You uphold the way of honest and faithful souls. Your judgment rests upon those who destroy. As for me, I will trust in You, El Shaddai.

---

56. Mortal: O God, be merciful to me. I am surrounded by those who want to harm me because of my trust and loyalty to You. So great is their determination that they constantly oppress me. In my fear, I put my trust in You, my strength. And so my fear subsides, for I know that Your promises are firm. With You, how can others harm me? Others make trouble for me all day long. They always seem to be trying to hurt me. They stalk me, watching all that I do, hoping they can somehow harm me. I pray, O God, that your revenge will rise up and do away with their constant scheming. You know how troubled I am, for I know You keep track of all my tears; they are all listed in Your book of care. I am confident, O God, that in Your time and Your way, You will hear my prayer and answer. It is in Your promises. I trust in You, and my fears subside. With You, how can others harm me? O God, I offer You what I have promised; it is my song of praise and thanksgiving to You. You rescue me from defeat and disgrace. And so I walk in Your divine presence, bathed in the light that brings life to all mortals.

57. Mortal: O Saving God, be merciful to me! In the shadow of Your wings, I find protection, until the raging storms are over. I call to You, Most High, because You supply my every need. You, El Shaddai will answer and save me. You will defeat my oppressors. You will show me Your constant love and faithfulness. I am surrounded by vicious predators, snarling at me with fire in their eyes. I pray that You will show your gentle power and Your judgment over all the earth. Others have spread a net to catch me. I am overcome with distress. Sometimes they get caught in their own traps. Even now, I have complete confidence in You, O God. I will sing and praise You! With the instruments that I play, I will fill the day with gladness. I will sing songs of thanksgiving and praise among the people. Your constant love is high, reaching beyond my sight. Joy will come when all will know of Your greatness and wonder, flooding over them.

58. Mediator: You leaders of nations, do you ever rule with justice? Do you judge everyone fairly? No! You think only of the wrong you can do. You commit crimes of violence in the land. From the beginning you have ruled wickedly. You are deaf to the One who created all people. You do not hear the voice of wisdom and justice.

Mortal: O God, break the power of these poisonous predators. May they be washed away in Your cleansing flood. Trample their wayward and violent ways. May the worst ills that I can think of visit their souls, for I know that You are a righteous and just God.

Mediator: The faithful and good folk will rejoice when they know that the oppressors are punished. They will dance in the places left empty by the violent. The faithful and good are rewarded for their constant trust in God, who judges the world with truth.

---

59. Mortal: Protect and save me, O God, from those who know only violence and corruption. These bloodthirsty bandits crouch in the shadows, seeking to harm me. Are they present now because of the wrong I have done? Is this a punishment for my many faults? Rise up, Sovereign God, and come to my aid. You know what they are doing. Punish those who harm me for no reason. In the evening they prowl like hungry dogs. Do You hear their insults and threats? Their words harm me, and they think that no one else can hear them. But You do hear them and laugh at their ignorance. Saving God, I have confidence in Your strength. In Your love, You will see and hear what is happening and defeat the wrong.

Mediator: Do not kill the haughty ones, O God, or the people will forget Your power. Scatter them by Your strength and defeat them.

Mortal: O God, our protector, sin is on the evildoer's lips. All their words are arrogant and wrong. Because they curse and lie, let Your anger defeat them completely. Then everyone will know that You, O God, are Sovereign over all principalities and powers, even death itself. Even if the wicked return, snarling like dogs once more, roaming about like hungry beasts, I will not be afraid. I will sing about Your strength. Every day I will sing aloud of Your constant love. You have been a refuge and a shelter in times of trouble. I will praise You, my protector and safe home. I will praise Your great love.

---

60. Mortal: You have rejected us, God, and defeated us. You have been angry with us. Turn back to us now. You have made the land tremble, and You have wounded it. Bring healing, for we are falling apart. You have made Your people suffer greatly. We stagger around as though we were drunk. You have warned those who have reverence for You that they might escape condemnation. Save us by Your might. Answer our prayer. May the people You love be rescued.

Mother: From on high I will divide the nations and deliver portions for the good and faithful. The whole world belongs to Me. And those who dishonor Me will be humiliated. I discern who have been faithful and true, and who have turned their backs on My Commandments and ways. When I have finished, everyone will know of My justice.

Mortal: Who will take me by the hand and lead me to safety? Have You rejected all of us, O God? Aren't You going to defend us as You have in the past? I look at the helpless around me and pray to You, O God, our only help. Only You can provide the strength and protection that we need.

61. Mortal: Hear my prayers, El Shaddai, and listen to my cries. I call to You in my despair, far from home. Embrace me in Your safe-keeping, for You are my protector. You give me courage and strength in times of trouble. Let me live in Your safe home all my life. Like a baby chick, may I hide under Your protecting wings. You have heard my promises, El Shaddai, and You have granted to me what You give to those who honor You. I also ask that You strengthen the lives of faithful servant leaders, so they may live to serve a long time. May their service be filled with justice and integrity honoring You, and being compassionate to the lowly and poor. Let them always know of Your love and faithfulness. So I will always sing praises to You, while I offer my service as a daily sacrifice.

62. Mortal: I wait patiently for El Shaddai to save me. I depend on Her alone. She alone protects and saves me. She is my defender, and I shall always live in safety.

Mediator: How much longer will all of you attack one lowly soul, who is no stronger than a broken-down fence? Your only goal is violence and dishonor. You take pleasure in lies. While you speak words of blessing, your hearts are filled with curses.

Mortal: I depend on El Shaddai alone. I wait patiently for Her alone. She alone protects and saves me. She is my defender, and I shall always live in safety.

Mediator: Trust in El Shaddai at all times, O people. Tell Her all your troubles, for She is your protection. Mortals are all like a puff of breath. Great and small alike, they are worthless. Put them on the scales, and they weigh nothing. They are lighter than mere breath. Don't put your trust in violence. Don't hope to gain anything by robbery. Even if your riches increase, don't depend on them.

Mortal: More than once, I have heard El Shaddai say that power belongs to Her and that Her love is constant. I am sure that She rewards everyone according to our deeds.

63. Mortal: O God, You are my God. I constantly seek to be close to You. My whole being desires Your presence. I am like a dry, worn-out, and waterless land. My soul is thirsty for You. Let me know of Your presence in Your holy place. Let me see how strong and beautiful You are. Your constant love is better than life itself. So I will sing praise to You. I will give You thanks as long as I live. I will raise my heart to You in prayer. Because of Your abundance, I will feast and be filled in my soul. I will sing glad songs of praise to You. In my bed, I remember You. All night long, You are in my heart and mind. You have always been my help. In the shadow of Your wings, I sing for joy. I cling to You, and Your gentle strength keeps me safe. Others who wish to harm me will fail; they will become powerless. They will meet the fate they wanted for me. They will be no more.

Mediator: Because God is Sovereign, the faithful will rejoice. Those who live in God's Covenant will always sing God's praises. But the mouths of the liars will be shut.

64. Mortal: Listen to my prayer, O God, for I am deeply troubled. I have so many fears that I fear for my very life.

Protect me from the violence of others. They speak awful words that hurt like sharp knives. Others quickly spread shameless lies. They destroy the good and humble folk with cowardly slander. They group together in their low and uncivil plans. They think they are working in secret where no one can see. They conspire for the perfect crime. Why do they find any purpose in this?

Mediator: God overpowers these oppressors. God destroys their plans and takes away their strength and influence. God has heard their words. The faithful and just will be in awe over all that God can do. They will rejoice because of God's great strength. They will put their trust in God, always giving God praise and honor.

⸻

65. Mortal: O God, it is good for me to praise You in this holy community. Because You answer our prayers, I will keep my promises to You. I join others everywhere who come to You, confessing great sins. If we do not confess, we are brought very low. But You forgive sin. Happy are those who bathe in Your blessings, who live close to Your holy place. We shall be satisfied with Your abundance and blessings. You answer our prayers and Your strength saves us. People all over the world trust in You. We can see Your strength in the mountains and the power of the roaring waters. With this same strength, You calm the uproar of the peoples. Many are in awe of Your greatness and power. When we consider Your presence, we shout for joy. From all directions, people gather to praise Your great works. In Your tender care, the rain falls on the land, making it rich and fertile. The streams are filled with the water that provides life for our crops. You send abundant rain on the plowed fields and soak them with water. You soften the soil with showers and cause the young plants to grow. Your goodness provides the rich harvest. Your nurturing presence assures that there is plenty. The pastures, too, are filled with grazing flocks. The hillsides are filled with joy. The fields are covered with the goodness of Your provision. All creation sings for joy!

---

66. Mediator: All you people, praise El Shaddai with shouts of joy. Sing to Her, offering wonderful praise. Say to Her, "How wonderful are all Your accomplishments. Your strength is so great that all others are in awe of You. Mortals from all over bow down and worship You, singing Your praises." All People, see the wonderful acts among you that El Shaddai has accomplished; Her wonderful acts among you. Remember how your ancestors were able to cross the waters as on dry land. They were filled with joy in their safe passage. El Shaddai is Sovereign over the nations. Assure that others do not rise against Her. So praise Her, all peoples; let your praise be heard above the tumult. We are alive because of Her care and protection.

Mortal: You have put us to the test, El Shaddai. As silver is purified by fire, so You have tested us. You let us fall into a trap, and have placed heavy burdens on our backs. You let others overwhelm us. We have experienced fire and floods. But You also brought us to a place of safety. We will offer our greatest sacrifices, as we have promised. We will give You what we promised, in times of trouble. All of the greatest offerings will be given You. Come and listen, all who honor El Shaddai. We will tell of Her great accomplishments. We

others be completely frustrated. May those who are trying to hurt me be shamed and disgraced. I will always put my hope in You. I will praise You more and more. I will live in a way that others will know of Your goodness. My words will be of Your saving graces, even though they are beyond my understanding. I will praise Your strength, Sovereign God. I will reflect Your goodness, Yours alone. You have taught me since I was a child. I still live in the truth of these teachings. Now that I am old and my hair is gray, O God, do not abandon me. Be close to me while I live in the light of Your blessings and grace. Let these be known to the generations that follow me. O God, Your righteousness reaches great heights. You continue to accomplish great works. There is no other greater than You. Though You have let me see trouble and suffering multiply, I am sure that You will strengthen me. I trust that my journey will continue in peace. So I will continue to praise Your presence and faithfulness, O God. My soul will be filled with hymns of praise to You, filling my whole being with songs of hope and strength that come from You. I will reflect Your righteousness, which has been my companion all my life. I will rejoice, for those who wish to harm me have lost their power.

—

72. Mediator: Give the gift of justice to all those who lead, O God. May all who rule over others know of Your righteousness. May all those who are governed enjoy prosperity that honors You. May all leaders have mercy on the poor, helping the needy and defeating those who would oppress them; may all people ascribe great worth and value, above all else, to You, O God, day and night. May servant leaders rule like gentle rain that blesses the land. May justice and peace flourish in this life time; may prosperity, which honors You and Your Creation, last forever. Above all, may Your will and way prevail both near and far, over all people. For You deliver the poor and needy and all those who trust in You. May Your justice be found on all the continents and on the far-flung islands of the sea. May all who lead humbly follow Your will and way. You hear those who cry out to You. You rescue those who are needy and rejected, those who suffer oppression and violence, for they are precious to You. May Your servant leaders live and rule a long time. May their many gifts honor You. May the people know simple abundance, may the cities teem with faithful and honest folk. May prayers continually honor You; may You be known in all nations because of Your faithful servant leaders. May all know that You alone are Sovereign, and may they praise Your gentle strength. Let it always be so!

73. Mediator: God is good to those who have a pure heart.

Mortal: I had nearly lost confidence in God. My faith was almost gone. I was jealous of the arrogant and self-centered when I saw them prosper at the hands of others. They do not seem to suffer any pain. They appear strong and healthy. They do not seem to have the afflictions and troubles that others have. They are disgusting in their violent and hardhearted ways. Their lives are filled with plans to oppress the lowly. They look at ordinary folk in a way that dishonors God; they laugh at them. The haughty seem so powerful and successful that ordinary folk eagerly follow their example. They see this and think that God does not have any idea of all that they do to destroy communities. Those who have more than enough only seek to get more. I wonder if I have been a fool for remaining faithful. O God, why is there so much suffering and brokenness now? In my faithfulness, why am I suffering? I cannot figure out what You want of the faithful people like me! I know I will enter into a place where I know You, O God, can be found. I will seek to know what will happen to the egotistical and corrupt . . . Your healing Word rests upon me! I now understand. Those whom I envy have no foundations. Though they prosper now, they are doomed by their own wickedness. The day will arrive when they will disappear like the morning fog. For You, O God, are Sovereign over all principalities and powers, even death itself. Now I know that my envy of these proud and self-centered people was low and a waste of time. I did not understand Your gentle presence. When I stay close to You, I find You guiding me with Your present will and way. I am reminded that I only need to seek Your honor and Your presence. I do not need anything else. Those who abandon Your ways have only themselves. Then they discover their emptiness and weakness. So I will always seek Your safe home. I will always praise Your great love.

74. Mortal: Why have You abandoned us like this, O God? Will You always be angry with Your faithful people? You chose us long ago, remember? You brought us out of slavery to belong to You alone. You spoke to our ancestors in fire and smoke. But now, all that we have held as sacred is destroyed. Those who dishonor and reject You seem to have prevailed. We have seen them demolish all that we hold as belonging to You, O God. We have seen Your holy place go up in flames. All our sacred symbols are gone. All those who speak Your word are silenced. No one knows how long we must endure this disaster. O God, how long will we be humiliated like this? Even You are being dishonored. Why do You seem silent and helpless? You are the Sovereign One, always able to help. We remember when You led our ancestors through the deep waters. Your strength prevailed over great odds. You made water gush from hard rocks in the dry deserts. At other times You made the earth parched and dry. All of creation is of Your design, setting the rhythms of our lives into seasons, days and nights. Do You hear that these narrow-minded people laugh at You and dishonor Your creation? Make Yourself known among Your helpless people. Give us power over the cruel and violent oppressors. We remember the Covenant we have with You. In this time of violence and destruction, do You remember it? Don't let the lowly, broken, and outcast be put to shame. Strengthen the poor and needy, so we can lift our voices in praise to You. Let the laughter and anger of the destroyers stir You to action.

75. Mortal: El Shaddai, we give You thanks. We proclaim how great You are and tell of all Your wonderful accomplishments.

Mother: I have set a time for justice to prevail, and I will judge with fairness. Let every mortal fall to their knees in awe, for I can shake the very earth. I warn the conceited not to be arrogant. I tell them to cease their self-centered ways.

Mediator: Justice is not reserved for mortals from any-where. It is El Shaddai who is the judge, who condemns and forgives. El Shaddai is filled with rage against the unjust. She overcomes those who dishonor Her Creation and all that is in it. They will not rise again.

Mortal: I will always speak of the God of my ancestors, sing-ing praises to Her. Her gentle strength will overcome the bigoted and corrupt. But the power of the good and faithful will grow stronger.

——

76. Mediator: God's people are very familiar with El Shaddai. They know that She can be found where there is justice and peace. They know that Her presence makes all places holy. The weapons of war fizzle in Her presence. The strength of those clad in armaments wilts when She speaks. When She shows Her strength, there is no other power that can match Her. Though slow to anger, Her righteous rage brings others to their knees; it is more powerful than when the earth quakes. Her judgment brings the rattle and violence of conflict to complete silence. Her justice provides safety for all who have been oppressed. The faithful will praise Her more, even when violent souls lift their voices in anger. The survivors of wars and civil unrest vow to celebrate Her fes-tivals. All people, fulfill your promises to El Shaddai. Make great sacrifices that honor Her throughout the nations. Faithful souls, worship Her. Great leaders, be humbled in Her presence.

——

77. Mortal: Does El Shaddai hear me when I cry? In times of trouble, I pray to Her. All night long I lift my hands in prayer. But at times, I do not find comfort. These are times when I sigh deeply. My meditations bring only discouragement. My worries keep me awake all night. I think of days gone by and remember years long ago. In my bed, I wonder if El Shaddai will always see only the wrong we have done and never rejoice in our faithfulness. I ask if She has stopped loving us. Have our misdeeds cancelled Her promises to us? Has She forgotten to be merciful to us? Has Her silence taken the place of compassion? Then I wonder if She has lost Her strength. But other days and other nights, I remember all the great and wondrous deeds El Shaddai has accomplished. I will meditate on them with great thanksgiving. Now my prayers are much different. I remember the holiness and greatness of El Shaddai. She works miracles, showing Her strength near and far. Her redeeming strength brings safety to the faithful people, as She has for their ancestors. All of Creation tells of Her power and compassion. Great storms remind us of her strength. Her presence can be found even on tiny boats far from land. She has called forth faithful servant leaders to show people the way.

***

78. Mediator: Listen, all people, to my teaching, and pay attention to what I say. I am going to use wisdom to explain mysteries from the past. You have heard in them the teachings of our ancestors. They are to be passed on to our children, so the next generation will know of El Shaddai's power and great acts, in all Her wonderful accomplishments. She gave laws to our ancestors in faith and Commandments to their descendants. They were to teach these laws to their children so that generation would learn them and in turn would tell their children. In this way, all generations would put their trust in El Shaddai and remember to obey Her Commandments. Then they would not be like other rebellious and disobedient people, who did not really trust in Her and did not follow in Her way. In time of conflict they were not confident, for they knew of their failure to keep the Covenant and their refusal to obey Her laws. We remember the waters parting and passing through the tumult, as on dry land. We remember Her leadership in fire and smoke. We remember water spurting from solid rocks and streams coming from the arid places. Others remembered these also but continued to turn their backs on El Shaddai, rebelling against Her in the wilderness. They deliberately put Her to the test by demanding the food they remembered from slavery. They doubted that She could respond. They challenged her to provide bread and meat in the wilderness. This angered El Shaddai, for these bitter people did not believe that She could save them. Then the miracles began to happen. And every morning She provided enough bread for every household to be satisfied. And in the evening, She stirred up the winds that brought the faithful and unfaithful alike enough meat for them to be satisfied. But even then, the bitter and rebellious people did not trust Her. In Her anger, many of them perished in the wilderness. When the others saw what was happening, they repented of their rebellion and turned to Her in prayer. They remembered the strength of the One who had saved and watched over them. But these were empty words. Their actions showed they were not loyal to Her and to Her Covenant. But El

Shaddai was compassionate and forgave their mistrust. She held back what they deserved, remembering they were only mere mortals, no more than a spring breeze. This happened often in the wilderness. These wandering and lost people continued to put Her to the test again and again. They forgot Her saving power and the many miracles. They forgot the many plagues She visited upon their oppressors in Egypt when their rivers turned into blood so there was no water to drink. They forgot the plagues of flies and frogs and locusts. They forgot the hail and frost that killed the crops of their oppressors in Egypt. They even forgot the Passover, when the first-born of theirs were saved and all others perished. They forgot being led through the desert and the raging waters. They even forgot how El Shaddai had provided them homes in a land filled with great abundance and safety as She had promised. Still these precious people rebelled against Her. Still they put Her to the test and did not obey Her Commandments. Like the generations before, they were disloyal and unworthy of Her love. When they had settled, they found of value all sorts of idolatry that had nothing to do with their Sovereign God. This was disastrous, for El Shaddai abandoned them, and they lost the power to protect themselves, and many perished. This lasted while homes were destroyed and families devastated. Even the priests were not protected from Her rage. When the time of punishment for all their rebellion was over, El Shaddai was present once more. Peace returned to the faithful people. This time She selected a new family of leaders who could be more faithful. And from this family arose the humble servant, David, who would build the people to a strong and peaceful nation.

79. Mortal: O God, people who we do not know and do not understand are all around us. Their way of life seems to desecrate all that we hold as holy. Our cities are in ruins; and some people have been left in the streets to die. There are so many dead that there is no one left to bury them. Other nations insult us, laugh at us, and mock us. Sovereign God, will You be angry with us forever? Will our lives be consumed in fire? Why don't You punish those nations who don't worship You as we do and do not pray like we pray? Don't You see what they are doing to us? Are You punishing us for the sins of our ancestors? We are losing hope; have mercy on us! We ask that You rescue us and save us from this desperate time. Forgive our sins, so others will not think You have abandoned us. Already others are asking, "Where is your God?" Be present in defeating those who have shed our blood. Release all those imprisoned and who are condemned to die. Visit upon these invaders Your ultimate vengeance. Then we, Your humble children, will lift our songs of thanksgiving and our prayers of praise to You, O God.

80. Mortal: Sovereign God, listen to us and hear the groaning of our souls. Show us Your strength and save us! We have been scattered to the far reaches of the world. Bring us home. Will You not listen to our honest prayers? You have given us sorrow to eat and a large cup of tears to drink. You have let others inhabit what we call ours. We experience great insults. Bring us home, Sovereign God. Show us Your mercy and save us. You are the God of the Passover and the Promised Land. We flourished in the abundance of our new land. We were like a lush vineyard that flourished and provided our needs. But now You have stopped protecting it from passersby and anyone who will steal from its generous harvest. Even wild animals trample what is left. Remember us, Sovereign God. Show us Your strength and compassion, so we may be saved. Restore the vineyard of Your delight, for it has been cut down and burned with fire. Punish all those who have destroyed what You have called precious. Preserve and protect all those whom You have chosen for Your own. This time we humbly promise we will never turn away from You again! Save our very lives, and we will always trust only in You. Bring us home, Sovereign God, and we will know of Your mercy and peace.

81. Mediator: Shout for joy to God our defender. Sing praises to the God of our ancestors. Begin the music of praise and thanksgiving, playing joyfully on Your instruments. Blow the bright trumpets during the great festivals, recalling how merciful and protecting God has been.

Mother: I took the burdens off your backs. I let you put down your heavy loads. When you were in trouble, you called to Me, and I saved you. Deep within the power of a storm, I answered you. I put you to the test when water gushed from solid rock. Listen up, you people whom I love. You must never worship another god, or give your allegiance to any other power. I am the One who brought you out of slavery. Open your mouths and I will feed you. But you do not listen to Me. Therefore you do not obey Me. So I let you go your stubborn ways and do whatever you want. How I wish you would listen to Me and obey Me. Then your troubles would end, and your heartache would be no more. Those of you who have turned your backs on Me, and ridiculed the faithful, would be punished for your arrogance and self-centered lives. But I would feed the faithful and just with the finest of foods, and they would be satisfied.

---

82. Mediator: El Shaddai presides in the highest council and speaks to Her people.

Mother: Your injustice must stop. You must no longer deny the poor and outcasts their fair judgment. Defend the rights of the lowly and rejected. Be fair to the needy and the helpless. Rescue them from the harm that the haughty and bigoted do to them. How ignorant you are. You are completely corrupt, and justice cannot be found anywhere. In My love, I raised you above all other creatures, being next only to Me. But you will perish, for you have not honored the blessings I have given you.

Mediator: O El Shaddai, rule all people, and let your justice be found in all nations.

---

83. Mediator: O God, do not be quiet. Don't let Your silence continue, when there is so much turmoil. Those who despise You are growing stronger. They are plotting against the people You have protected for so long. They plan to destroy the faithful and just, so that goodness will be forgotten. They are making alliances with others to build on their strength. Even those who were overwhelmed in the past are growing stronger against You. It may be that they wish to claim for themselves the very Promise You have made.

Scatter them like dust, O God. Let Your response to them be like a raging forest fire. Let them find themselves in the midst of a powerful storm and terrifying winds. Cover their faces with shame, O God, and make them acknowledge Your power. May all their plans wither and die. May their strength be no more than a breath of air on a hot day. May the arrogant and self-satisfied learn that You are Sovereign over all principalities and powers, even death itself.

84. Mortal: O God, I deeply desire to always be close to Your presence. With my whole being, I sing for joy, for You are still speaking. Even the sparrows have built nests, as have the swallows. They keep their young close to You, our Creator. Happy are those who live close to Your presence. Their strength comes from You. Even when they find themselves in the wilderness, You provide springs of water and still pools of refreshing water. They grow stronger as they journey on the pathways close to You. Hear my prayer, Sovereign God. Listen, O God of my ancestors. Be with all Your blessed servant leaders! One day spent in Your presence is better than a thousand anywhere else. I would rather stand near Your Holy Presence than live in the homes of people who reject and make fun of You. For You are our Sovereign Protector. You bless us with kindness and integrity. You do not refuse to bless with goodness all the faithful and just. Sovereign God, how happy are those who trust in You!

85. Mediator: Sovereign God, You have been merciful to Your land and have made it prosperous. You have forgiven

Your people's sins and pardoned all their wrongs. You have stopped being angry with them, and You have held back Your furious rage.

Mortal: Bring us home, O God our Savior. Stop being displeased with us! Will You be angry with us forever? Make us strong again and we will praise You. Show us Your constant love, and give us Your saving help.

Mediator: I am listening to the Sovereign God, who is promising peace to the people. But you must not return to your foolish ways. Salvation will be assured to those who honor God. You will live once more surrounded with beauty, abundance, and peace. Love and faithfulness will meet. Justice and peace will embrace. Faithfulness and trust will rise up. God's righteousness will flow down from on high. The land will yield abundantly, and God will help you prosper. God's goodness will bring safety, joy, and peace.

---

86. Mortal: Sovereign God, I pray that You hear my prayers. I am helpless and near to death. Save me, for I am Your loyal servant, and I trust in You. Be merciful to me, the God of my whole life. You know that I am constant in prayer. Grant me gladness, O God. I pray these prayers, for I know that you are forgiving and full of constant love. Listen, Sovereign God, to my cries for help. I am in times of deep trouble. You are Sovereign over death itself, O God. You are Sovereign over all principalities and powers. There is no other greater and more powerful than You. You are known in all nations because of Your justice and strength. People near and far have witnessed Your awesome deeds. Teach me, O God, what You want me to do, and I will faithfully obey You. Show me how to serve You with total devotion. I will continue to praise You with all my heart, Sovereign God. I will radiate Your constant love at all times, for You have saved me from the grave. The egotistical and narrow-minded ones, who pay no attention to You, rise up against me, and I fear for my life. I pray to You, O God, for You are merciful, loving, always patient, always kind, and faithful. My prayers are for Your mercy and strength to save me. I have always served You as my mother did in her life. Make visible Your goodness in my life so those who bear down on me will be ashamed. Show them Your comfort and help toward me, saving God.

87. Mediator: The Sovereign God builds mighty cities and makes them holy. Within their boundaries, God can always be found. Teeming cities, filled with great diversity, are a delight to God.

Mother: Because I have given birth and watch over all people, I know very well those who are faithful and obedient. They are found in all nations throughout all Creation. In their life journeys, they find themselves living in great cities. This gathering of all peoples is of My design. My delight is in these vast communities, and I will make them strong. I keep track of where My people live. It is My joy that there is a mixture of all the nations within great cities. They belong together as neighbors. They will dance together and sing their songs. It will be the source of great blessing.

88. Mortal: Saving God, I cry out all day and all night in prayer to You. Listen to my cry for help! So many troubles have fallen on me that I fear I will die. My strength is gone. I feel abandoned, as if I am already dead and lying in my grave. I feel as if You have forgotten me completely and that I am beyond Your help. It seems as if You have thrown me into the region of tombs where there is no light. The silence of Your anger crushes me like a heavy load. Even my friends have abandoned me. I am repulsive to them. I am trapped in this turmoil, and my eyes can see nothing but suffering. Saving God, every day I raise my heart and soul to You in prayer. Do You perform miracles for the dead? Do they rise up and praise You? Can Your constant love be spoken in the grave? Is Your faithfulness found in places of destruction? Are Your miracles seen when there is no light? Does anyone know of Your goodness in the land of the forgotten? Saving God, I call to You for help. I begin every morning in prayer. Why do I know only Your rejection? My whole life has known great suffering and trial. I am worn out by the burdens of what seems to be Your punishment. I am crushed to the point of destruction. Is this Your anger? All day long, I am surrounded and flooded by these troubles. I am without anyone who cares for and supports me. Silence and loss are my only companions.

89. Mortal: Gentle God, I will always sing of Your constant love. I will live in witness to Your faithfulness forever. I know that Your love will last beyond my life and that Your faithfulness is as permanent as the sky.

Mother: I have made a Covenant with My chosen servant leader. I will depend on a lineage of faithfulness, integrity, and trust in Me to lead people and nations in justice and peace.

Mortal: The heavens sing of Your wonders and faithfulness, Sovereign God. You have no equal in all Creation. Even in the meetings of great leaders, Your wisdom and way are held high. All people live in awe of You. You are faithful in all ways, Sovereign God. Your power can be seen in the great force of storms. You crush monstrous chaos and scatter Your foes. If we look in any direction, near and far, we see Your presence and strength. You are known through righteous, justice, and lasting peace. Love and faithfulness enrich all that You do. Happy are the people who know of Your great worth. They sing songs of joy. All day long they rejoice in Your goodness and kindness. You give us the ability to prevail over great heartache and turmoil. You have lifted up great servant leaders whom You lead with Your Spirit.

Mother: I have helped those who are courageous and strong. I have raised them to places of leadership. I have made them My servants, anointing them with holiness. My strength will always be with them; it will be their strength. They will be able to prevail over great odds. The arrogant and violent people will not rule over them. They shall have leadership over the far reaches of Creation. They will know that I am their God. I have given them birth and will always watch over them. I will always keep My promises with them, and My Covenant with them will last forever. Their influence will be remembered for many generations. And their descendants will lead. But I lay upon them great responsibility. All these servant leaders and their descendants, any upon whom the responsibility of leadership falls, must obey My laws. They all must live by My Commandments. If they disregard My laws and do not live by My Commandments, I will punish them and will make them suffer for all that they have done that does not honor Me. I will not stop loving them or fail to keep My Promise. I will not break My Covenants. I will always speak truth to them, and I will watch over their communities for all time. I can lift My anger at My chosen leaders. It will be as though I have deserted them and broken My Covenant with them. Great troubles will occur then, with great cities being destroyed and looters dividing the spoils. I can raise up enemies to accomplish My directives. I can make your defenses useless. I can take away any respect you may have enjoyed and cover you with disgrace.

Mortal: Sovereign God, when You punish us, will You hide Yourself forever? How long can Your anger burn like fire? My life is very short; all of us are only mortals. Will we live to see the signs of Your love? How will I know of Your promises? Do I have to endure the punishment intended for others? Your enemies insult Your servant leaders wherever they go. Help me to praise You forever, Sovereign God.

90. Mortal: Sovereign God, You have always been our home. Before You created the hills or brought the world into being, You were eternally God and will be God forever. You call us to return to You. When we die, we become dust. A thousand years to You are like one day. They pass quickly and are gone. You carry us away like a flood, and we last for only a moment. We are like weeds that sprout in the morning, flower in the heat of day, and dry up by nightfall. We are destroyed by Your anger and are terrified by Your fury. You know our sins, even our secret sins that we try to hide. Our life is shortened by Your judgment, and we fade away. Seventy or eighty years are all we can expect to live. During our lives, we experience trouble and sorrow. Life is soon over, and we are gone. Who alive knows of Your rage? Who knows the number of our days? Teach us how short our life is, so that we may become wise. How much longer will we suffer in this life? Have pity, merciful God, on Your servants. Fill us each morning with Your constant love. Let us sing and be glad all our life. Give us now as much happiness as the sadness You gave us. Let us, Your servants, see Your mighty deeds of forgiveness and healing. Let following generations know Your peace. Sovereign God, we ask Your blessings upon us, and help us prosper.

91. Mediator: Those who seek the Sovereign God for safety and protection can celebrate that God is their defender in whom they trust. El Shaddai will keep you safe from all hidden dangers and all serious troubles. She will cover you with Her wings, and you will be well cared for. She will protect you with Her faithfulness. You need not fear any dangers at night or sudden trouble during the day, or the feared plagues, or any evil that threatens your life. You will be secure even though many around you are troubled. You will be able to see how the proud and careless are punished. You have made God your companion, who will be with you in times of trouble. Therefore, your home will be spared of violence. El Shaddai will provide angels to be with you in your journey. They will hold you up and keep you from stumbling. You will be safe from predators.

Mother: I will save those who love Me. I will protect those who trust Me. When they call to Me, I will answer them. When they are in trouble, I will be with them. I will rescue them and honor them. I will reward them with a long and peaceful life.

---

92. Mortal: How good it is to give thanks to You, Sovereign God, to sing in Your honor, O Most High God. How good it is to proclaim Your constant love every morning and Your faithfulness every night, with the music of many instruments. Your mighty deeds, O God, make me glad. Because of all You have accomplished, I sing for joy. Your actions reflect thoughts beyond our understanding. The fools and those who reject You grow like weeds. Those who harm others may prosper, but they are always within Your power. You will make them suffer as they have afflicted others. We know they will be defeated. Your faithfulness has made me strong. You have blessed me with happiness. I know that You are just, with me and all others. The good and faithful will flourish like trees by a flowing stream. They grow embraced in Your nurture and protection. They continue to bear good fruit for many years and are full of life. This reveals Your justice and goodness, O God.

---

93. Mediator: The Sovereign God is wrapped in majesty and strength. The world has been created and cannot be shaken. God's presence and power have been from the beginning, existing far beyond our memory. The ocean depths cause us to praise God, raising our voices over the roar of its waves. God can be found in all of Creation. God's power is greater than all other powers. God's laws are eternal. Mortals will always know a holy place where God can be found.

---

94. Mortal: God of justice, reveal Your judgment. Rise and let Your justice fall on the arrogant and self-satisfied. How much longer will they be glad? How much longer will the corrupt boast about their crimes? They crush the poor and outcast. They do great harm to those whom the world has forgotten, and murder the strangers in our midst. They say that You do not see them and You do not care.

Mediator: How can you faithful be so stupid? When will you ever learn? El Shaddai can hear just as you can. She can see what you see. She is powerful over all people and is just. She knows what all people are thinking. She laughs at all these thoughts and actions.

Mortal: El Shaddai, happy are those to whom You teach Your law. You give them rest from days of trouble. You watch as the greedy dig the pits that will catch them. El Shaddai will not abandon Her people. She will not desert those who trust Her. Justice will again be found in the courts. All good and faithful people will rejoice. But at times, I have wondered, who stood up for me against the oppressors? Who took my side? If El Shaddai had not helped me, I would surely have suffered greatly. I cried out, God, I am falling! And I found myself supported and embraced by a wonderful love. I am comforted and content even in times of anxiety and worry. I am sure that You reject corrupt judges who make injustice legal, who plot against the good and sentence the innocent to death. El Shaddai is my defender. So great is Her justice that She will punish the wicked according to their deeds.

95. Mortal: All people, let us sing for joy to El Shaddai, our protector. Gather in Her presence with thanksgiving, singing songs of praise. For She is Sovereign over all principalities and powers, even death itself. She rules over all Creation. Let us bow down before Her and kneel humbly in Her presence. She is our Creator and Savior, and we are the people She lovingly guides and nurtures.

Mother: Don't be as stubborn as your ancestors once were. Even though I had accomplished great miracles, they still tested Me in the desert to see what I would do for them. I was so disgusted with them that I let them wander in the wilderness for forty years. They were disloyal. They refused to follow My commands. I made a solemn promise that none of them would enter the land I had promised them.

96. Mediator: Sing a new song to El Shaddai, all people! Sing and proclaim every day the good news that She has saved us. Proclaim Her glory and wonderful accomplishments to others. El Shaddai is great and is to be more highly praised than all other powers and principalities. She is the Creator of the whole world, and there is no other God. Her presence is filled with strength and beauty. Revere Her above all false powers and values, above all the phony idols that others think are great. Let all your lives be an offering of faithfulness and service to El Shaddai. Be in awe of Her gentle and ever-present love. Live in such a way that many others will know Her wonders and miracles. Her Creation is firm and dependable. She loves all people justly and fairly.

Let all Creation rejoice, as in a great celebration. Let all people rejoice in the peace that Her justice brings!

97. Mediator: Be glad, all people. El Shaddai is Sovereign over all Creation. She rules with righteousness and justice. She is the fire that purges evil. We know Her strength in the lightning and thunder of great storms. When the earth is shaken, we rejoice in the power of Her Creation. We have only to look up to the heavens to know of Her beauty and wonder; it is available abundantly to all people. Those who put great hope in lifeless images and ideas are put to shame. Only El Shaddai is worthy of praise. Let all families and cities, all clans and tribes, rejoice in the gentle strength of Her judgments. She is the ruler of all Creation, and there is no other God. She loves all those who turn their backs on greed and bigotry. She protects the lives of faithful people and rescues them from the clutches of the oppressor. Radiance and gladness shine on the faithful and good. Be glad for all that El Shaddai has accomplished. Every day, remember Her Peace with thanksgiving.

98. Mediator: O Sing a new song to El Shaddai, who is wonderful in all Her deeds. She has prevailed with Her gentle strength. So wonderful are these accomplishments, which are known among all people. She keeps Her promises with the people of the Covenant. She shows loyalty and constant love for them. And all people know of Her care. Sing for joy to El Shaddai, all people. Praise Her with songs and shouts of joy! Let your songs of joy sound from instruments great and small. Let all Creation be a sign and celebration of Her love. Clap your hands, all people; sing together of your joy! El Shaddai is Sovereign over all the people. She rules with justice for rich and poor alike.

—⋙—

99. Mediator: All people are in awe of the Sovereign God. From on high, God's gentle strength can shake the earth. God's presence is found near and far and can be found in all nations. In their own way, all people praise God.

Mortal: Sovereign God, You love all that is good. You have established justice among Your people. You have brought justice to rich and poor alike.

Mediator: Praise to God, who is holy on high. Our ancestors were called to serve God. When they prayed, God answered them, speaking at times from the pillar of a cloud. They obeyed God's laws and commands.

Mortal: Sovereign God, You answered Your people. You demonstrated that You are a forgiving God. In Your just love, You even punished them for their sins. Let us praise and bow down in awe before You, Holy God.

—⋙—

100. Mediator: Sing to God, all Creation! Bow down in humble awe before God with joy. Enter into God's presence with joyful songs! All mortals were created by, and belong to God. We are God's delight. God watches over us, protects us, and provides for us. Approach God's presence with thanksgiving. Live aware of all that God does in our lives, and be grateful. God's love is good, and lasts for all times. God's faithfulness will be with us forever.

101. Mortal: I will sing out songs of obedience and justice to You, O God. I will discipline my self to act as in Your sight. For me, and those who live under my roof, I will never tolerate greed, bigotry, arrogance, or untruthfulness. I appeal to You about the actions of those who turn their backs on You, O God. I will have nothing to do with them. I will have no dealings with the dishonest and unjust. I will reject anyone who whispers deceit or plans to do harm to another. I will not tolerate those who take advantage of the poor and profit from their oppression. I approve of those who are faithful to Your ways, O God, who humbly serve You. I will welcome them into my home. I will rejoice in serving others with them. No one who misrepresents the truth or says one thing and then does another will be a close friend of mine. Let my life reflect Your justice and Covenant. Let all those who do not honor You in their lives suffer the heartache they visit upon others.

102. Mortal: Listen to my prayer, Sovereign God, and hear my cry for help. I am in trouble now. Don't be silent. Help me to know how You can be with me now. My life is disappearing like smoke. My body is burning like fire. I am beaten down like dry grass, and I am no longer eating. I groan out loud. I am nothing but skin and bones. I feel abandoned like a bird that has lost its way in the wilderness. I lie awake and can only think of all those who have insulted and cursed at me and have mocked me to my face. Your silence seems like anger that tastes like ashes in my food. My tears mingle with the little that I drink. It is as though You, O God, have thrown me away. The light of life is fading from my days. But You, Sovereign God, are present to all generations. You rise and take pity on all those who suffer. Has the time arrived to show mercy? All Your servants love You. You have shown pity on many who have suffered greatly. Your grace and gentle strength are known throughout the nations. Even Your servant leaders know of Your healing power. In times of disasters great and personal, You are known to have listened to and answered prayers, in Your time and Your way.

Mediator: Write down for the next generations what the Sovereign God has accomplished. Let those not yet born learn to praise God. From on High, God hears the groans of the prisoners and sets free those who were condemned to die. Honor God's will near and far, in small communities and great cities. This will bring healing.

Mortal: God has made me weak while I am still young. I fear I will not live much longer. O God, do not take me away now, before I grow old. You are eternal. You created all there is. But the earth, and everything in it, is only temporary; we will wear out like clothes. Only You will remain. You are constant and Your presence will never disappear. The next generations will live in safety, under Your protection.

---

103. Mortal: Praise El Shaddai, my soul! All my being, praise Her holy love. I will remember Her kindness. She forgives all my sins and heals all my diseases. She keeps me from the grave and blesses me with love and mercy. She fills my life with abundant goodness and health.

Mediator: El Shaddai judges in favor of the oppressed and gives them justice. She revealed Her plans to our ancestors; and Her mighty deeds in the wilderness. El Shaddai is merciful and loving, slow to become angry and full of constant love. She does not keep on scolding and is not angry forever. She does not punish us, as we deserve, or repay us for all our sins and omissions. Her love is as high as the sky above the earth. Those who have reverence for Her know of Her love. As far as the east is from the west, so far does She remove our sins from us. Her loving kindness is reflected in those who parent well. She knows our character and remembers that we are mere mortals. We are like grass, growing and flourishing like wildflowers. Then the hot winds blow; we wither and are gone. Those who honor El Shaddai know that Her love lasts forever and Her goodness endures for all generations. Those who follow Her commands and are true to Her Covenant rejoice in Her presence among all people. She is Sovereign over all people and is present in all nations. She is to be praised by all who obey Her commands and listen to Her still small voice. She is to be honored by all servants, of high and low standing, who do Her will. All people, near and far, honor and praise Her presence with all Your soul and strength.

---

104. Mortal: Praise to You, Sovereign God, O my soul. Your greatness, majesty and glory radiate light to all people. Your heavens are spread out like a tent; from there, the rains fall. Clouds race across the sky, riding on the wings of the wind. Your winds are Your servants, and lightning is Your messenger. All Creation is on sure foundations. The oceans reach far and wide and are deeper than the highest mountains. The power of Your Creation can make the waters flow out to sea and rush back again. Springs burst forth in the valleys, and rivers run between the hills. They provide water for the thirsty beasts and mortals alike. Trees are a safe place for birds and other creatures to raise their young. The earth is blessed with rain that falls on crops and pastures, providing food for all creatures. We are assured of abundant wine and oils to make us cheerful, and the bounty of the land. All trees and animals find their own places in Your Creation. Some seek out the high mountains, while others build their homes near rushing rivers. We measure time by the sure rhythm of moon and sun. In Your Creation, there is enough for all. You provide a delightful variety and abundance beyond our imagining. You are outrageously generous in all Your provision, O God. All this shows the wisdom and perfection of Your Creation. We will never know or even see all the countless designs in Your Creation, all that reflect Your delight and humor. Each in its own way depends on You, O God. You are the provider of daily food. When you turn away, all creatures can suffer and die. You bring us forth, and our lives have breath. May Your glory last forever! May You continue to delight in Your Creation. May Your power continue to touch large and small alike. I will sing to You, the Creator, all my life. As long as I live, I will sing praises to You, O God. May You be honored in all that I do. May justice fall on those who despoil and greedily take more than their share from Your abundance. May polluters and wasteful people stop dishonoring Creation and You, O God; praise to You, the creating God, O my soul!

105. Mediator: Give thanks to El Shaddai and proclaim Her greatness. Let all people know of Her goodness. Sing praises, telling of Her wonderful acts. Let all people bow down and honor Her, your Protector. Remember the miracles performed in the midst of your ancestors. And remember Her judgments. El Shaddai's commands are for all people. She keeps Her Covenant forever, Her promises to thousands of generations. Even the promises made centuries ago to your ancestors are the source of your blessings. Remember the story. Long ago, the ones who knew and followed Her lived in Canaan and were few in number. Even in their wanderings, they were kept safe by El Shaddai. In a time of great famine, the servant Joseph, a slave, was allowed to use his gifts to save the faithful. The people grew strong, and their strength caused them to be enslaved. Other servants, Moses and Miriam, were called to lead the people through many plagues and raging waters, through death and great miracles. They found a new freedom close to their Savior but far from what they knew. By fire at night and a cloud in day, the people were led out to safety. They were given bread to eat every morning and meat to eat every night. Water gushed from a rock. All the promises El Shaddai made, She remembered. Through the wilderness She led them. And they shouted and sang for joy. In Her time and Her way, She led them to a new place and a new home as She promised. All of these events and miracles were for one purpose: the grateful people would obey all Her laws and keep all Her commands forever! Praise to the Promise Maker and Promise Keeper!

106. Mediator: Praise the Sovereign God! Be grateful for God's eternal goodness. Who can tell of God's great accomplishments? How can we be as thankful as these miracles deserve? Happy are those who are obedient and who are always found doing good works. Remember God when you serve others and bring new hope to them. Let your prosperity and happiness be shared with faithfulness.

Mortal: We have sinned as our ancestors did. We have forgotten God and gone our own ways. Our ancestors long ago did not understand God's wonderful acts. They did not remember the many times they were loved in miraculous ways. They rebelled against the Almighty at the Red Sea. But God's promises saved them in order to show God's great power. God commanded the Red Sea to part and the people crossed, as on dry land, saving them from their oppressors. When a powerful army followed them, the sea returned over the pursuers and drowned them all. Not one survived. Then our ancestors believed in God and sang out loud praises. It wasn't long before they found themselves wandering in the desert. They were filled with craving in the desert, and they did not remember all that God had done. So they tested God, asking for food and water. And God gave them what they asked for. But God also punished them for forgetting. Many experienced diseases. Then many became jealous of God's chosen servant leaders. The people who acted this way were punished also in an earthquake and in fire. Our ancestors did not remember their God when they made a gold idol and worshipped it. They exchanged the glory of God for the image of an animal that eats grass. They forgot God, who had saved them through great miracles. God's anger flared to destroy these people. But Moses pleaded to save them, and they were saved. Then our ancestors did not believe and rejected God's promises and would not listen to God. God saw this and warned them that they would all die in the desert and their descendants would know no faith community. Then our ancestors began worshipping the God of fertility and broke many laws of their faith. God saw this, and our ancestors experienced a terrible disease that broke out among them. Then one servant knew the justice that must occur and punished those who offended God. Again our ancestors did not follow the laws set forth for them; they did not maintain the purity of their faith and adopted other ways of believing, even worshipping lifeless idols. They even offered their own children as sacrifices to these lifeless idols. They killed innocent children, and the land was defiled by these murders. They made themselves impure by their actions and were unfaithful to God. God saw this and was disgusted and angry with our ancestors. So God gave up on them and let them be ruled by those who did not know God. They were severely oppressed by their captors. In God's own time and way, our ancestors were eventually rescued. But they chose to rebel again and sank further into sin. When they finally cried out to God for help, God heard them and took notice of their distress. For their sake, God remembered the Covenant. Because of great love, God relented from their punishments and filled their oppressors with compassion. Save us, Sovereign God, and gather up Your scattered people. Save us so that we may be thankful and praise You, redeeming God. That we may praise You, God, now and forever! May it always be so.

107. Mediator: Give thanks to God whose goodness and love are eternal! Repeat these words often, remembering

Mediator: Remember your ancestors, who were defeated and humiliated by cruel oppression and suffering. God showed contempt for their oppressors and made them wander in the trackless deserts. God rescued the needy from their misery and made their families prosper. The faithful and good see this and are glad. But all who do not honor God are silenced.

Mortal: Thank the Sovereign God whose goodness and love are eternal! May those who are wise remember God's constant love.

---

108. Mortal: I have complete confidence in You, O God. I will sing and praise to You! I will wake up and play on my instruments, O my soul. In the morning, I will thank You, O God. I will praise You among the people. Your constant love reaches above the heavens. Your faithfulness touches the skies. Continue to show Your greatness on high, O God, Your wonder is everywhere we go. Save us by Your might. Answer my prayers of intercession, so that others You love may be rescued.

Mother: By My strength I will provide lands and cities for My people. I will lift them up, and I will punish those who do not serve Me. Over those who are My enemies, I will proclaim victory.

Mortal: Who, O God, will take me into this mighty city? Who will lead me by the hand? Or have you rejected us, O God? Have You decided to withhold Your strength in times of our turmoil? Help us in our conflicts, O God. Mortals are worthless at times like these. With You on our side, O God, we will have the strength to overcome these challenges.

109. Mortal: I praise You, O God. Don't remain silent. The vicious liars attack me, saying untrue tales about me, for no reason. They do this even though I love them and have prayed for them. They pay me back evil for good and hatred for love. I want You, O God, to choose some corrupt judge to try these awful people, so they get a taste of the justice they use to harm me. May they be tried and found guilty of even the prayers that they offer. May they be driven away and other people assigned to work in their place. May their children become orphans and their marriages fail. May their family become homeless beggars, and be driven from the ramshackle places where they live. May their creditors take away all their property and strangers get everything they worked for. May no one ever be kind to them or care for the family members that are left behind. Then may all their descendants die and their names be forgotten in the next generation. May You, O God, remember their evil and never offer forgiveness. For those who oppress me, have never thought of being kind. They are like this with all the poor, the needy, and the helpless. May You curse those who love to curse. May no one bless those who refused to give blessings, for they curse as naturally as they dress themselves; may their own curses soak into their bodies like water and into their bones like oil; may their own curses cover them like a blanket and always be around them like a belt. O God, I want You to punish my enemies in that way, for they are so cruel to me. O God, help me as You have promised and rescue me because of the goodness of Your love. I am poor and needy. I am hurt to the depths of my heart. Like an evening shadow, I am about to vanish. I am blown away like an insect. My knees are weak from lack of food. I am nothing but skin and bones. When others see me, they laugh at me, shaking their heads in scorn. Help me, O God, because of Your constant love. Make those who harm me know that You are the One who saves me. Though they curse me, may You bless me. May they be defeated, and may I rejoice. May they be covered with disgrace and wear their shame like a robe. Then I will give loud thanks to You, O God. I will praise You in the assembly of the people. You defend the poor and humble and save us from those wish to harm us. Thanks be to You, O God!

110. Mother: O servant leader, sit close to Me, and I will make you prevail over great odds. Even when you are in greatest conflict, you will find people coming to your side. Like dew in the early morning, there will be those who will surround you and support you, for you are My servant. Your gifts honor and serve Me. Therefore I will give you the vision of My vision so that you may speak with My words in the way of the greatest of leaders before you.

Mediator: El Shaddai will always be close to you. Her fury will strengthen you when you confront greed and injustices. She will pass judgment on all people and will prevail over all situations. Her influence will prevail far and near. She will renew you and strengthen you in your service.

111. Mortal: With all my strength, heart, and soul, I will thank and give praise to El Shaddai. How wonderful is all She does! Everyone who delights in Her accomplishments seeks to understand them. All She does is full of honor and beauty. Her righteousness is forever.

Mediator: El Shaddai does not let us forget Her wonderful actions. She is kind and merciful. She provides good food for all those who know of her love and honor Her. She never forgets Her Covenant. She has shown Her gentle strength to all people by providing for them a land in which to live and a safe home. All She does is faithful and just. All Her directions are dependable. Her commands will last for all time. They were given in truth and faithfulness. She set Her people free and made an eternal Covenant with them. Holy and powerful is She! By having reverence for El Shaddai, all people will become wise. She gives sound judgment to all who obey Her. She is to be praised forever.

112. Mediator: Give praise to the Sovereign God. Happy are those who have reverence for God and enjoy obeying God's commands. Their children will be leaders in the land and their descendants will be blessed. Their households will prosper. Light shines everywhere for the faithful, for those who are merciful, kind, and just with rich and poor alike. Happy are they who are abundantly generous in life and run their businesses honestly. They will be remembered for their successes for a long time. The faithful souls are not afraid of receiving bad news, for their faith is strong, and they trust in the Sovereign God. The gracious, compassionate, and just do not fill their lives with worry and fear, even in times of great trouble. Their kindness continues, even in tough times. They will be known in this way because of their strength. The hard-hearted and unjust will become angered because of them, but their threats will come to nothing. Their hope to dominate will be an empty wish. The Sovereign God is just and merciful.

⁓⟨≋⟩

113. Mediator: Give praise to El Shaddai. You servants of El Shaddai, praise Her now and forever. From the rising of the sun to its setting, give Her praise. She is known in all nations and Her Commandments are followed by many people. There is no other god like El Shaddai. From on high, She embraces all of Creation, large and small. She raises the poor from the dust and lifts the needy from their misery. She places them among the powerful and makes them leaders from their humble beginnings. She gives the despised women a home and calls them to nurture children in need. Praise to El Shaddai!

⁓⟨≋⟩

114. Mediator: When our ancestors were rescued from slavery in a foreign land, they were aware of how blessed they were. It was God who parted the raging and flowing waters. It is God who can make the mountains and hills dance in great celebration. How do the great waters become dry land? Why do the mountains skip and jump as if by command? Be in awe, all people. God is very close. The God of your ancestors is not far away. The same God, who can change rocks into pools of water and solid cliffs into flowing streams, is still present!

⁓⟨≋⟩

115. Mortal: Do not give glory to us, El Shaddai. To You alone must all glory be given because of Your faithfulness and constant love, even when other people ask us, "Where is your God?"

Mediator: El Shaddai is on high and is Sovereign over all principalities and powers, even death itself. Other people have gods they have made of silver and gold. These gods have mouths but cannot speak, and eyes that cannot see. These idols have ears but cannot hear, and noses but cannot smell. They have hands but cannot touch, and feet but cannot move. May all who made and trust in them become as empty and lifeless as the gods they worship; trust in El Shaddai, you blessed people. She helps you and protects you. Trust in El Shaddai, all Her messengers. She directs and nurtures you. Trust in El Shaddai, all you who pray and give praise to Her. She is your help and hope. El Shaddai remembers you and will bless you. She will bring joy to all faithful households, faith communities, and Her messengers She has called. Her joy will be upon all those who honor Her, the rich and poor alike. May El Shaddai grant these blessings on all generations of your household; may you be blessed by the Creator and Redeemer of all the world. She is on high and has given us the earth to bless and care for. We do not know how the dead can praise El Shaddai. But you, the living, will give Her thanksgiving and praise for ever! Glory be to El Shaddai!

116. Mortal: I love El Shaddai because She hears me when I pray, and listens to me when I call out to Her. The danger of death was all around, with the horrors of the grave closing in on me. I was filled with fear and anxiety. Then I fervently prayed to El Shaddai to save me. She is merciful and good. El Shaddai is compassionate. She protects the helpless and saves me from danger. Be at peace, my heart, because of Her goodness. El Shaddai saved me from death and stopped my tears. In faith I walk in Her presence as I go about life. I kept on believing even when I felt completely crushed, afraid, and un-trusting. What can I offer to El Shaddai for all Her goodness to me? I will bring great offerings in thanksgiving for her care and protection. In the assembly of the faithful, I will offer Her all I have promised. It must be painful to Her when a servant dies. I am Your servant, El Shaddai. I serve You, just as my mother did. You have saved me from death. So I am offering You a sacrifice of thanksgiving and my grateful prayers. In the assembly of all Your faithful people, in Your presence, I will offer all that I have promised. I praise You, El Shaddai, because of Your abundant love.

117. Mediator: Praise the Sovereign God, all nations! Praise God, all peoples near and far! God's love for us is dependable and strong. God's faithfulness will last for all time. Give praise to the Sovereign God!

118. Mediator: Give thanks to El Shaddai, for She is good, and Her love is eternal.

Mortal: El Shaddai's love is eternal! Her love lasts forever! Her love will never end! In my distress I called to Her, and She answered me and set me free. El Shaddai is with me, I will not be afraid, for no one can harm me. She helps me when I am in conflict with others. It is better to trust in El Shaddai than to depend on mortal leaders. When I was in conflict with others to the point of desperation, She gave me strength. They swarmed around me like bees, but Her presence was like a raging fire. El Shaddai gives me strength in conflict. Let the faithful communities sing in joyous thanksgiving for Her deliverance. I will live serving Her. She grants me hospitality to enter into Her presence with thanksgiving with other good and faithful people. She is the cornerstone of faithful communities. But some do not understand and reject Her. Her transforming actions are marvelous in our eyes! This day, and every day, has dawned because of Her, let us celebrate. Happy and blessed are those whose journeys in life are filled with the memory of Her goodness and love. With holy symbols we will dance in Her presence. You are holy, El Shaddai. I will give thanks and live out what You have called me to do.

Mediator: Give thanks to El Shaddai, for She is good and Her love is eternal.

119. Mediator: All those who are obedient to El Shaddai's laws are happy. All those who follow Her commands with their hearts are blessed. They avoid disobedience in their faithful journey through life. El Shaddai has given Her laws and told all to obey them faithfully. Be earnest in keeping Her instructions! Pay attention to all Her commands. Then you will not be put to shame. Learn Her righteous judgments, and praise Her with a grateful heart. Obey Her laws so She will not abandon you.

Mortal: Boys and girls learn early to obey the Commandments and be blameless. With all my heart I try to serve El Shaddai and pray for Her to keep me from disobedience. I keep Her law in my heart so that I will not sin against Her. Teach me Your ways, El Shaddai. I recite by heart Your commands and delight in following them. It is more satisfying than being wealthy. I study Your instructions and seek the deep meanings of Your teachings. I take pleasure in Your laws. I will not forget them!

Mortal: Compassionate God, be good to Your servant so I may live and obey Your teachings. Open my eyes, so that I may see the wonderful truths in Your law. I am here on earth for just a little while. Do not hide Your guidance from me. My heart deeply longs to know Your judgments at all times. You punish the arrogant and curse those who oppress the poor and outcast. Free me from those who insult me and heap scorn on me for obeying Your laws. Powerful people whisper against me as I study Your teachings. I trust Your instructions with pleasure. They show me Your way.

Mortal: Defeated in the dust I lie, O God. Revive me as You have promised. I have confessed all I have done. Answer me and show me Your ways. Help me to understand Your laws, and I will meditate on Your wonderful teachings. But now I am overcome by sorrow. Strengthen me, as You have promised. Keep me from going the wrong way; and in Your goodness, teach me Your law. I have chosen to be obedient. I have paid attention to Your judgments. I have followed Your instructions, O God. Don't let me be put to shame. I will eagerly obey Your commands, for You will give me more understanding.

Mortal: Eternal God, teach me the meaning of Your laws, and I will obey them my whole life long. Explain Your laws to me and I will obey them and keep them close to my heart. Aid me in being obedient to Your Commandments, for I find great happiness in them. Give me the desire to obey Your laws rather than to trample others, while trying to get rich. Keep me from paying attention to what is worthless in life. Show Your goodness that You have promised. I, Your servant, pray that You keep the promises You have made to those who obey You. In Your wonderful judgments, save me from the insults I fear. I want to obey Your commands, so I may have new life from You, righteous One.

Mortal: For the affirmation of Your promises, show me that You love me, O God. Then I can answer those who insult me, because I trust in Your Word. Enable me to speak the truth at all times. My hope is always in Your judgments. I will always obey Your law, forever and ever. I will live in peaceful freedom because I seek to obey Your teachings. I will make sure that even great leaders will hear Your commands, and I will not feel shame in doing so. I find pleasure in obeying Your commands that I love. I respect and honor all Your commands. I will meditate and study Your instructions.

Mortal: Great hope has been given me, O God. For I, Your servant, have remembered Your promises to me. Even in my suffering, I was comforted because Your promise gave me life. The arrogant are always scornful of me, but I have not departed from Your law. I remember Your judgments of long ago, and they bring me comfort, Sovereign God. When I see the greedy and bigoted breaking Your law, I am filled with anger. During my brief earthly life, I compose songs about Your commands. In the night, I remember you, O God, and think about Your laws. I find my happiness in obeying them.

Mortal: How can I ask for more, O God? All I want is to obey Your laws. With all my heart I pray that You have mercy on me, as You have promised. When I review my life, it is filled with promises to follow Your instructions. I do not hesitate to do so. The corrupt and violent have tried to trap me, but I remember Your law. In the middle of the night I wake up to praise You for Your righteous judgments. I seek to be a companion of all who are Your servants, of all who obey Your laws. Sovereign God, the earth is full of Your constant love. Teach me Your way.

Mortal: In Your goodness, O God, You have kept Your promises to me, Your servant. Give me wisdom and knowledge, because I trust in Your commands. Before You punished me, I used to do wrong. Now I obey Your word. How good and kind You are! Teach me Your commands. The haughty ones have told lies about me. Yet in my heart, I have Your instructions. The corrupt and violent have no understanding of this. But I find pleasure in Your law. My punishment was good for me, because it made me learn Your commands. The law You gave means more to me than all the money in the world!

Mortal: Just as You have created me, O God, You have kept me safe. Give me understanding, so that I may learn Your laws. Those who have reverence for You will be glad when they see me, because I trust in Your promises. I know that Your judgments are righteous, Sovereign God. And You punished me, because You are faithful. Let Your constant love comfort me, as You have promised me, Your servant. Have mercy on me, and I will live. I take great pleasure in Your law. May the proud be ashamed for all they do. As for me, I will meditate on Your instructions. May those who have reverence for You join me, so we may grow in Your wisdom together. May our souls be blameless in keeping Your word. May we never be put to shame!

Mortal: Knowing that even when I am weary, O God, I can trust in Your word, and You will save me. When my eyes are tired of watching for what You have promised, when I ask for You to help me, when I feel as useless as a discarded container, yet I do not forget Your commands. How much longer must I wait for You to punish those who harm me for my faith? The self-important, who do not obey Your law, have tried to trap me. Your Commandments, O God, are all trustworthy. Help me when others try to harm me. They have almost succeeded in doing away with me, yet I still remember Your commands. Be good to me, out of Your constant love, so that I may live obeying Your laws.

Mortal: Loving God, Your Word will last forever and ever. Your faithfulness endures through all the ages. You have ordered all Creation. Everywhere I look, I see the signs of Your reliable Creation. If Your ways had not been the source of my joy, I would have died from my sufferings. I will always remember what You have taught me, because by them You have kept me alive. I am Yours; You have saved me! I always seek to be obedient to You, even when many predators are trying to harm me. Even in times like these, I study and meditate upon Your laws. In life there are many limits, but Your Commandments are perfect and potent.

neglect Your teachings. Your righteousness will last forever, and Your law is always true. When I am filled with trouble and anxiety, Your Commandments bring me joy. Your instructions are always just. Give me understanding, and I will live.

Mortal: Save me, O God, when I call to You with all my heart. Answer me and I will always follow Your commands. Before the sunrise, I call to You for help, as I place my hope in Your promise. All night long, I lie awake to meditate on Your instructions. Because Your love is constant, O God, I pray that You hear me; show me Your mercy and preserve my life! Those who wish to harm me, because of my belief in You, those who never keep Your law are closing in on me. But You, O God, are even nearer to me. Your ways are my strength. Long ago I learned about Your teachings. They are eternal!

Mortal: Too long I have been suffering, O God. I have not neglected Your law! Defend my cause and set me free, as You have promised. Those who have no time for seeking Your will are far from Your help and concern. But Your compassion, Sovereign God, is great. Even when there are many troubles for me, I do not fail to obey Your laws. I am disgusted with those who totally deny Your love and justice. But look at me and see how I love Your instructions. Your love never changes; so I pray that You will save me! The heart of Your law is truth, and all Your judgments are eternal.

Mortal: Unjust people surround me, O God. But I respect Your law. How happy I am because of Your promises. I am as happy as someone who finds rich treasure. I love Your truth and wisdom, but I despise my self-deception. Seven times each day I thank You for Your righteous judgments. Those who love Your will are blessed with great peace. They do not stumble over the obstacles in their path. I wait for You to save me, Sovereign God, so I can continue to obey You. I love Your teachings with all my heart. I obey Your commands and Your instructions with all my strength. You know I live this way.

Mortal: Very early each morning, I cry for help to You, O God. Give me understanding as You have promised. Listen to my prayer and save me according to Your will. I will always praise You, because You teach me Your laws. My lips will sing praises of Your justice. I will make Your desires my delight. I will praise You for renewing my soul. I will trust in Your mercy to help me. Come looking for me, O God, for I have lost my way. Find me, for I continue to obey You.

> NOTE: This meditation, in its original form, was probably written beginning each paragraph with the twenty-two letters of the Hebrew alphabet. You are invited to write your own meditations beginning with the last four letters of the English alphabet.

120. Mortal: When I was in trouble, I called to El Shaddai, and She answered me. She is the One who can save me from those who lie and deceive others. How will El Shaddai deal with such people? How will She punish them? There are many ways, and some of them involve great pain. How great a challenge of faith it is to live among those who are corrupt and violent. How difficult to be neighbors with those who have given up on a hope for peace. El Shaddai, when some people think that war is the only way, help me to speak peace, live peace, teach peace and be at peace with others and with You!

---

121. Mortal: Will I find any help or safety from defenses in the mountains? No. My help and safety come only from El Shaddai, who made all Creation.

Mediator: El Shaddai will not let you fall. Your Protector is always awake. The guardian of all faithful people never dozes or sleeps. She will watch over you. She is by your side to shelter you. You will not be hurt while the sun shines in the day, nor will any danger come to you when the moon shines at night. El Shaddai will protect you from all peril. She will keep you safe. She will watch over you as you go about your daily life, now and forever.

---

122. Mortal: I was glad when I was invited to enter into God's holy presence and to be within this mighty city.

Mediator: This great city is being restored to beautiful order and harmony. All people of all tribes and races gather. They are grateful to have had the wisdom to follow God's commands. Here great decisions are made that affect many people. Pray for tranquility within this city. May all the faithful prosper; may there be calm within these boundaries, and peace within all families. For the sake of all whom we know, neighbors and strangers, travelers who know no homes, may peace rest upon them all. For the sake of the households of faith and all servants of the living God, I pray for abundant peace.

123. Mortal: El Shaddai, I look to You, on high. As an employee depends on his boss and an infant depends on her mother, so we will keep looking to You, gentle Leader, until You have compassion on us. Be sympathetic to us, Redeemer, and be merciful to us. For we have been mistreated by many who have shown contempt for us. For we have been mocked too long by the rich and hardhearted, and scorned by selfish oppressors.

124. Mortal: What if El Shaddai had not heard our cries for help and answered us? What would have happened if Her strength was not greater than those who have abused and overwhelmed us? We would have been swallowed in the flood of their passion; carried away as in a raging river. We would have been hidden in the foaming torrent, far from those who could have saved us from drowning. Blessed be El Shaddai, who has saved us from those who harm us. We are free, like those who have sprung the hunter's trap. El Shaddai is our helper! She has created us and sustains us.

125. Mediator: Those who trust in God are like the high mountains, which cannot be destroyed, nor can they be moved. As the mountains surround the fertile valleys, so God surrounds all Creation. God will remove all corruption and injustice, making whole the homes, cities, and nations where people dwell. God will keep the faithful from dishonoring the Covenant. But those who insist on acting, as though they were the highest authority, will be forgotten and abandoned to their own foolishness. May God's justice and peace dwell among all people.

126. Mortal: When God brought us back to our homes, it was like a dream! How we laughed and sang for joy. All those who knew what had happened agreed that the Sovereign God had accomplished great miracles. God took us back home like the rain that brings water back to dry riverbeds. And those who wept, as they planted their crops, will harvest the abundance with joy. Those who despaired as they went out, carrying their precious possessions, will return singing for joy in the midst of plenty!

127. Mediator: If God does not build this house, the work of its builders is for nothing. If God does not protect this city, it does no good for sentries to stand guard. It is foolish to anxiously work so hard for a living, getting up early and going to bed late, forgetting all else. For God provides, and all we need is ours in abundance. Children are a gift from God and a real blessing. They grow steady and strong to pass the heritage of goodness and faithfulness to another generation.

128. Mediator: Happy are you who have reverence for El Shaddai, who live by Her commands. Your work will provide for your needs, and you will live in abundance. Those in your household will be fruitful in their undertakings. There will be joy at the table, and life will be enriched each time you gather. All households who obey Her laws will surely be blessed in this way. May El Shaddai bless you with holy living; may you prosper with all Her people as long as you live. May the fruit of your nurture and direction be passed along in faithful adults, living in justice and peace!

129. Mediator: Oh, persecuted one, tell me how you have been treated for believing in God.

Mortal: Ever since I was young, I have been teased and abused for my belief. Even though others treated me cruelly, I was not overcome. At times I was deeply wounded, scarred to this day. But God has freed me from the slavery of those who mock God. Now I wish for vengeance over all those who hate faithfulness. May they all be like grass, growing where the soil is not deep; they will dry up and be carried away. No one will ever notice that they have lived. They will never receive a blessing.

130. Mortal: Out of the depths of my despair, I cry out to You, O God. Hear my cry for help! If You kept a record of our sins, we would all be condemned. But You forgive us, so that we should reverently obey You. I wait eagerly for You, O God, in whom I trust. I wait more eagerly than night sentries wait for the dawn.

Mediator: Faithful people trust in God, whose love is constant and whose saving grace is abundant. God will save all people from their sins!

131. Mortal: Sovereign God, I have given up my self-satisfaction and turned away from my arrogance. I do not want to walk in ways too difficult for me, nor do I want to understand heavy deep thoughts. Instead, I am content and at peace. As a child who is quiet in a mother's arms, so my soul is at peace within me. With Your people, I trust in You, now and forever, O God.

132. Mortal: Sovereign God, do not forget Your servant leaders and all the hardships they endure. Remember their vows to serve You in leading others. Deep within their hearts they wish to make You part of all their deliberations and decisions. We know of Your presence in our lives. We want to hold this high among the people. Let Your Holy Presence dwell within all our relationships forever. May Your servants do the good that honors You. May Your people shout for joy. Our ancestor in faith, King David, was promised that his inheritance, for all time, would be servant leaders of Your people. Where Your promise dwells in the hearts of leaders, there You have a home.

Mediator: God's home is within these servant leaders.

Mother: In the company of faithful people is where I want you to live forever. This is where I want My Commandments to bear fruit. I will richly provide for everyone's needs, and I will satisfy the poor with food. I will bless the servant leaders, and all the people will sing and shout for joy. I will establish a lineage of servant leaders who shall prevail in times of conflict. Their leadership will prosper and flourish.

133. Mediator: How wonderful it is, how pleasant, for all God's people to live together in peace. It is like the precious anointing of oil that runs abundantly and covers our whole heads. Peace is like the dew on the mountains and meadows of Creation. Peace is where God's blessings can be found, in all times, now, and forever.

134. Mediator: All servants of God, gather together in an assembly of praise. Sing with joy both day and night. Raise you hands in prayer in God's presence, with hymns of praise. May the God of Creation bless you from on high.

135. Mediator: Give praise to El Shaddai, all faithful servants who stand in Her presence. Praise Her because She is good. Sing praises because She is kind. She chose to love and care for your ancestors.

Mortal: I know that El Shaddai is greater than all other powers and principalities. All of Creation is the benefactor of Her delight. Stormy clouds and lightning, strong winds, and rain; all are signs of Her presence. We remember the miracles of the Passover in Egypt, and all times when She prevailed over others who did not follow Her way. El Shaddai, You will always be proclaimed as Sovereign over all generations. You will defend Your people, and will have compassion for Your servant leaders. Many others who either do not know You, or turn their backs on You, find other ways and other idols to worship. These are made of silver and gold by mortals. These idols have mouths, but cannot speak and eyes that do not see. These idols have ears that do not hear, and are in no way alive. May all who worship mere things become empty and lifeless as well.

Mediator: Praise El Shaddai, all people. Praise Her, all servant leaders. Praise Her, the least of the community; praise Her with all your hearts. Praise Her when you are far from Her presence, or very near. Give praise to El Shaddai!

136. Mediator: Give thanks to the Sovereign God, who is good; whose love is eternal. Give thanks to the One who is Sovereign over all principalities and powers, even death itself. God performs great miracles. God created the earth and deep waters, the heavens and the lights that flow from them. Through God's eternal love, the Egyptian captors experienced great plagues and allowed the faithful to flee, with death passing over their households. God led the people out of Egypt and through the Red Sea, as on dry land. But those who pursued them were swallowed up. Even mighty armies are helpless in God's presence. God's eternal love led the people through the desert to the Promised Land; there God's promises prevailed over great odds. The people were able to settle in to a new land, a land where Abraham and Sarah received the Promise. God was always present with all creatures, giving food and flowing water to those in need. Give thanks to the Sovereign God, whose love is eternal!

137. Mortal: There are times when we find ourselves by streams in strange lands. These are troubled times, filled with weeping and great sadness for our homes far away. With only the trees to shelter us, we find little comfort. Those who oppress us want us to sing the songs we remember from home. How can we sing songs they don't understand, songs that only bring us sadness? We have been gone for so long that we are forgetting how to sing and how to play our instruments. When we are alone, we must sing together so we remember our home and all that we left behind. We must sing to remember our loving God. Remember, O God, what happened as we fled our homes! Remember how destructive everything was. When we think of the vengeance that will come to our captors, we are satisfied.

138. Mortal: I thank You, Sovereign God, with all my heart. I sing praise to You, even in front of those who refuse to worship and praise You. I seek Your presence, bowing down to sing Your praises. Your constant love and faithfulness have shown that Your commands are from on high. When I call to You, I am strengthened with Your strength. Leaders of many nations praise You, Sovereign God. They know of Your promises and honor You. They too, will sing of all Your glorious accomplishments. Even in Your strength, You know and care for the lowly and forgotten. Though they try, even the arrogant and violent cannot hide from You. You keep me safe in times of trouble. Your strength is greater than those who try to harm me. You keep Your promises. O God, Your love is eternal. Complete the Creation You have begun.

139. Mortal: Gentle God, You have examined me, and You know me. You know all that I do. From far away, you understand all my thoughts. You see me, whether I am working, playing, or resting. You know all my actions. Even before I speak, You already know what I will say. You are all around me, on every side. You protect me with Your strength. Your knowledge of me is so deep that it is beyond my understanding. Where can I go to escape from You? Were I to go the highest heavens, I would find You there. Were I to descend into great depths, even there I would find You. Should I try to flee to earth's farthest reaches, even there You would be close to me, leading me. If I try to hide where no one can see, there are no hiding places from You. Your light is everywhere, radiant, seeking, finding! Your creation of me is a wonder. Silently, I was knitted together in my mother's womb. What a wonder is Your detail and delight. Even then, You knew I was there. My whole life is written in Your book of life. What a wonder is Your knowledge of me. It must be more than grains of sand. Early in the morning, I am still with You! Search me, O God, and listen carefully to the meditations of my heart. Test me to discern my integrity. Find out if there is any evil in me, and guide me in Your everlasting way.

140. Mortal: Sovereign God, save me from greedy and violent people. They are always stirring up trouble. They speak destructively, poisoning everything around them. Protect me, O God, from their power, from the ones who wish to harm me. Constantly, they try to trap me with their deceitful and nasty speech. I cry out to You, O God; hear my cries! I call to You, for I know Your strength and Your dependable protection. It is my humble wish that You do away with all who trouble me. Dispose of these cruel people! I plead with

You that they may be repaid more than double of all the harm they pour on others. O God, I know that You defend the cause of the poor and the rights of the needy. Let good and faithful people praise You once more. Let us live close to Your presence, Sovereign God.

141. Mortal: Listen to me, Sovereign God, when I call to You. Receive my prayer as incense; my uplifted hands as an evening sacrifice. O God, I am sorely tempted to say words that will hurt others and me. Keep me from wanting to do wrong. Lead me away from temptation. Narrow-minded and uncaring people are trying to enlist my help. Don't let me even eat with them! It is good when a loving and faithful person rebukes my behavior in kindness. But never let me value what violent people say. Hear the prayers I am praying now. Let my faithfulness prevail, so others will know that Your Word is true. Let the cruel be shattered like wooden chips. Sovereign God, I will always trust You. I seek Your protection, for my very life. Protect me from all the many temptations. Let those who seek to overwhelm me fall into their own traps, preserving me so I may serve You.

142. Mortal: I call to You, O God, pleading for Your help. You hear all my trials and troubles. When I am ready to give up, You direct me. Because of my faith, I have many who challenge me. At times I feel like I am alone; no one will walk with me to give me strength. O God, I cry to You for help. You are my defender and all I want in this life. From deep in despair, I call out for Your help. Save me from those who wish to overwhelm me. Free me from my distress. Then, when I am with a community of faithful people, I can praise Your goodness shown to me.

—◆—

143. Mortal: Righteous God, hear my prayer! Listen to my pleas, spoken in faithfulness. Don't test me anymore, for no one is innocent in Your sight. You know how people have pursued my soul, almost crushing me. From this prison, I despair and feel ready to give up. I remember the former days, thinking about all that You have accomplished. I bring to mind all Your miracles. I lift my hands to You in prayer. My soul thirsts for You like dry ground. Will You answer me, O God? I have lost all hope. Are You hiding Yourself from me? Will I be among those who die, needlessly? Remind me each morning of Your constant love, for I put my trust in You. My prayers go up to You. Show me what I need to do. My prayer is for You to rescue me for these troubles. You are my God; teach me Your will. Be good to me, and guide me on a safe path. Rescue me, O God, as You have promised. In Your goodness, save me from my troubles! Because of Your love for me, destroy the power of those who harm me, for I am Your servant.

—◆—

144. Mortal: Praise the Sovereign God, who protects me in times of trouble. God is the only real defender, shelter, and savior in whom I trust. God is Sovereign over all principalities and powers. O God, what are mortals, that You notice us and pay attention to us? We are like puffs of wind. Our days are like a passing shadow. O God, be present and let Your strength be known. Save me from these deep waters; rescue me from the power of those who never tell the truth and lie even under oath. Let me sing to You a new song, O God. Let me play joyously on my instruments. You assure that faithful servant leaders prevail as You did with Your servant David. May our children be like plants that grow up strong and beautiful; may our fields yield abundantly and our flocks and herds prosper. May there be no cries of distress in our streets. Happy are all places where peace and justice reign. Happy are those who trust in You, Sovereign God.

<hr />

145. Mortal: I will proclaim Your greatness, gentle God. I will always thank You. For You are awesome and mighty; I highly praise You. Your vastness is beyond my understanding. Your remarkable accomplishments will be praised from one generation to the next. All people will rejoice in Your wonderful acts. They will speak of Your wisdom and mercy. I will join with others in celebrating Your gracious deeds. They will tell of Your goodness and sing about Your kindness. You, O God, are loving and merciful, slow to become angry and full of constant love. You are good to people and have compassion on all Your Creation. Let us raise our voices in praise to You, O God, with thanksgiving. Let us sing of Your wisdom and mercy. Others will learn of Your loving compassion. Your grace and peace can be found in all generations. You are faithful to Your promises, and Your compassion is filled with goodness. You help those who are in trouble and lift those who have fallen. Mortals look hopefully to You, for You are their Provider. You give them daily food that is very satisfying.

Mediator: The Sovereign God is merciful and righteous in all ways. God is near to those who call with sincerity. God supplies the needs of those who honor the One who hears their cries and saves them. God is your Protector and Sovereign Power over all other powers. Praise God, and let all mortals rejoice in their Redeemer.

146. Mortal: Praise God, my soul! I will praise God as long as I live, singing hymns of adoration all my life.

Mediator: Don't put your trust in mortals, for they cannot save you. When they die, they return to the dust. On that day, all their plans are ended. Happy are those who follow the God of their ancestors depending on God, who gave birth to all Creation. God keeps promises and judges in favor of the oppressed, giving food to the hungry. God sets the prisoners free and gives sight to the blind. God lifts those who have fallen and loves the faithful and good people. God protects the strangers who live in this land and helps the forgotten and rejected. God ruins the plans of the violent and arrogant, the bigots and deceitful, the greedy and self-centered. God is Sovereign for all time. Praise God!

147. Mediator: Praise God! It is good to sing praise to El Shaddai. She is restoring the magnificent cities and returning people to their homes. She heals the brokenhearted and bandages their wounds. She knows the number of stars each night and calls them by name. Strong and wonderful is El Shaddai. Her wisdom cannot be limited. She raises the humble but crushes the plans of corrupt and violent people.

Sing to Her hymns of praise, playing joyfully on your instruments. In Her delight, clouds provide the rain that grows the plants that feed Her creatures. She does not delight in powerful weapons or brave soldiers. El Shaddai takes pleasure in those who honor Her and who trust in Her constant love. Give praise to El Shaddai, all cities and all nations. She is the One who watches over You and keeps You safe. She blesses your people. She dwells along your borders, and keeps peace among your neighbors. She satisfies you with good food. At Her command, miracles happen in Her time and Her way. In Her delight, all Creation is blanketed with snow and is decorated with frost. Her Creation can form the hail that falls like gravel. Her cold winds test everyone. In Her time and way, the ice melts, the winds shift, and the rivers flow again. El Shaddai instructs all people. Her laws bring order to life. She favors those who follow Her will and way. Praise God!

148. Mediator: Praise God! Praise El Shaddai, who lives on high. Praise Her, all Creatures. By Her delight, all of Creation exists. All whom She has created have found the best places for their lives, and there they will stay. Give praise to Her for all creatures in the sea, for all that falls from the sky, and for the strong winds that blow from everywhere. Let all Creation be a celebration and praise of Her delight. Let all mortals join together, leaders and the led, exuberant youth and the wise aged, members of all races and clans. Let them all praise El Shaddai. She is greater than all others, and her glory can be found in all Creation. She strengthens nations and households so that all faithful and trusting people will praise Her.

149. Mediator: Praise God! Sing a new song to El Shaddai. Praise Her in the assembly of faithful people. Be glad and rejoice because of your Creator. Let your praises rise in dancing and the sounds of many instruments. El Shaddai takes great pleasure in people who humbly honor Her. Let Her people rejoice in their good fortune and sing joyfully all night long. Let them shout aloud as they praise El Shaddai. Her Word accomplishes Her will in this world. She can punish people and nations. She can bind all rulers with demands of obedience. She requires justice from all those who have been chosen to lead. Her justice is a source of joy for all people. Praise El Shaddai!

150. Mediator: Praise the Sovereign God! Lift your praise in God's holy presence. Praise God's strength. Praise God for mighty and wonderful deeds. With the call of the trumpet, praise God with many instruments. Let them ring and thump, crash and sing; winds and strings, mellow and bold, all join together in a mighty song of praise! Let all living creatures join in this glorious celebration to Praise God!